Feasting and Fressing Gallagher Style

by Deb "DGall" Gallagher

compiled by:

Jane and Harvey Westley

Ed and Esther Gallagher

Joel Manon

Fair Page Media LLC
Springfield, PA

ISBN: 978-0-9989098-3-7

Copyright © 2019 Jane Westley, Harvey Westley, Edward Gallagher and Esther Gallagher

All rights reserved.

Dedication

We want to dedicate these recipes to all the great cooks in our family. We were raised with parents and grandparents who worked hard to put tasty meals in front of us. Many of us were lucky to marry spouses who added to our cooking knowledge and skills. We have great Irish, Italian, German and Mexican culinary backgrounds in our family.

We are blessed to have a very close family relationship. One of our traditions is a family gathering over the Thanksgiving Holidays. This initially started with Ed & Joyce Gallagher encouraging their children's families to return from the far corners of the USA to the family homestead for Thanksgiving. This evolved into their children hosting the Thanksgiving gathering. Now, the third generation is taking over the mantel of sharing their homes and cooking skills to stay socially connected with each other.

When viewing one of these family gathering our sister, D'Gall, commented, "It is obvious that none of the Gallagher Clan is starving so we must be enjoying a lot of good eating." D'Gall remembered many of her favorite meals and thought they should be documented and shared as a family legacy. She initiated a project to collect and share all the favorite recipes of the clan.

We have now finished D'Gall's project. We want to thank all the family members, who contributed to this collection. We hope these recipes will provide a legacy for future generations to remember all the great cooks in the family and enjoy the meals of their heritage.

Jane Westley & Ed Gallagher Jr.

Table of Contents

Appetizers 1

    Deb's Asparagus-Prosciutto Rolls 2

    Westley Bacon Wrapped Smokies 3

    Chicken Liver Paté 4

    Deb's Christmas Tree Roll-Ups 5

    Cocktail Bread Hors D'oeuvres 6

    Deb's Coconut Shrimp 7

    Deb's Crab Bombs 8

    Westley Deviled Eggs 9

    Westley Pickled Eggs and Beets 10

    Westley Scallion Cheese Roll-Ups 11

    Indian Kebobs 12

    Shana's PA Dutch Soft Pretzels 13

    Zack Pirtle's Spicy Hot Popcorn 15

    Westley Trail Mix 16

    Lisa's Cool Veggie Pizza 17

Beverages 19

    Brandy Alexander 20

    Cranberry Drink Garnish 21

    Ed Sr.'s Bourbon Eggnog 22

    Slow-Cooked Hot Chocolate 23

    Spring Lemonade 24

    Southern Sweet Tea 25

Dips 27

    Seven Layer Refried Bean Dip 28

    Deb's Clam Dip 29

    Crab Imperial with Red Pepper 30

- Cream Cheese Dip 31
- Whipped Lemon Ricotta Dip 32
- Mexican Dip 33
- Roasted Onion Dip 34
- Vidalia Onion Dip 35
- Supreme Pizza Dip 36
- Blue Cheese Dip 37

Breakfasts 39

- Brenda's Baked Oatmeal 40
- Joyce's Creamed Dried Beef 41
- Hearty Egg Burritos 42
- Wes' Egg Rollups 43
- Jane's Bananas Foster French Toast 44
- Lisa's Baked French Toast 45
- Waffle Hash Browns 46
- Potato Chip Omelet 47
- Grandma's Tips for Making light and fluffy Pancakes 48
- Orange Oatmeal Pancakes 49
- Esther Gallagher's Baked Pineapple Casserole 50
- Esther Gallagher's Pistachio Coffee Cake 51
- Poached Eggs 52
- PA Dutch Potato Pancakes 53
- Brenda's St. Patrick's Day Scones 54
- Pennsylvania Fried Scrapple 55
- Swiss Cheese Scramble 56
- Grammie Jane's Waffles With Pecan and Banana Syrup 57

Salads and Dressings 59

- Asparagus Tomato Salad with Crabmeat 60
- Brenda's Dressing For Macaroni or Potato Salad 61

Doris Yost's Caesar Dressing 62
Cole Slaw 63
Deb's Dijon Vinaigrette Salad Dressing 64
Hollandaise Sauce 65
Brenda's Hot Bacon Dressing 66
Brenda's Layered Salad 67
Mango Salsa 68
Carolina Shrimp Salad with Avocado 69
Tomato Salad 70

Crockpot Soups 71

Lisa's Broccoli Cheese Soup 72
Lisa's Chicken and Wild Rice Soup 73
Lisa's Creamy Corn and Potato Chowder 74
Lisa's Crockpot Mexican Green Chile Pork Stew 75
Westley Football Tailgate Chili 76
Proszkow Vegetarian Chili 77
Lisa's Santa Fe Cheese Soup 78
Lisa's Crockpot Tomato and Rice Soup with Pesto 79
Lisa's Turkey and Rice Soup 80
Westley Ham and Bean Soup 81

Soups and Stews 83

Lisa's Chicken Vegetable Rice Soup 84
Dutch Chicken Corn Noodle Soup 85
Edward J. Gallagher's Chicken Corn Soup 86
Clam Chowder 87
Westley Corn Chowder 88
Lobster and Corn Chowder 89
Ed's French Onion Soup *(Soupe à l'Oignon)* 91
Potato and Leek Soup 92
Seafood Gumbo 93
Sharon's Creamy Winter Vegetable Soup 94

- Brenda's Award-Wining Chicken Pot Pie 96
- Dough for Brenda's Award-Wining Chicken Pot Pie 97
- Cowboy Stew 98
- Barley Jambalaya 99
- Westley Mild Jambalaya 100
- Ed's Sausage Stew 101

Entrées: Beef 103
- Jane's Beef Bourguignon 104
- Beef Tenderloin Roast 105
- Beef Wellington 107
- Jason Kretchman's Grilled Asian Flank Steak 108
- Mom's Hamburger Bar-B-Q 109
- Bacon-Wrapped Meatloaf 110
- Pot Roast 112
- Standing Rib Roast (Prime Rib Roast) 114
- Esther Gallagher's Steak Stroganoff 116
- Veal Liver and Onions 117

Entrées: Fish and Seafood 119
- Jane's Coquilles Saint-Jacques 120
- Grandma Ida Gallagher Mumford's Crab Cakes 122
- Deb's Baked Scallops 123
- Carolina Low-Country Shrimp and Sausage Boil 124
- Jane's Pineapple Shrimp Boat 125
- Lisa's Shrimp Scampi 126
- Baked Lemon Butter Shrimp 127
- Sharon's Spicy Shrimp 128

Entrées: Irish Specialties 129
- Corned Beef and Cabbage 130
- Irish Stew 131
- Shepherd's Pie 132

Entrées: Italian Specialties 133
    Angel Hair Pasta With Lemon and White Beans 134
    Chicken Cacciatore 135
    Esther Gallagher's Eggplant Parmigiana 136
    Lasagna 137
    Esther Gallagher's Linguine With White Clam Sauce 139
    Marinara Sauce 140
    Peas and Pasta Shells 141
    Jane and Sharon's Spaghetti Carbonara 142
    Spaghetti Pie 143

Entrées: Pork and Ham 145
    Maple-Coated Bacon 146
    Sweetened Ham Roast 147
    Ham Tips 148
    Pineapple Glazed Ham 149
    Pork and Sauerkraut 150
    Maple Roasted Pork Terderloin 151
    Pulled Pork 152
    Honolulu-Style Spareribs 153

Entrées: Poultry 155
    Jane's Beer Can Chicken 156
    Broccoli and Chicken 157
    Lisa's Chicken and Corn Pie 158
    Esther Gallagher's Chicken Gismonda 159
    Aunt Marta's Chicken Potato Chip Casserole 160
    Chicken Fajitas 161
    Lebanon's Firehouse Chicken 162
    Turkey or Tofu Tacos 163

Potatoes and Starches 165
    Baked Potatoes 166
    Esther Gallagher's Hash Brown Potato Casserole 167
    Mashed Potatoes 168
    Jane's Potato Salad 169
    Joyce's Old-Fashioned Warm German Potato Salad 170
    Lisa's Potato Spears (A Baked French Fry) 171
    Crispy Smashed Potatoes 172
    Drunken Coconut Rice 173
    Scalloped Potatoes and Chives 174
    Wild Rice and Savory Mushrooms 175
    Macaroni and Cheese 176

Vegetables 177
    Mom's 5-Bean Salad 178
    Ed's Baked Beans 179
    Brenda's Calico Beans 180
    Tammy Bly's Broccoli Casserole 181
    Baked Cabbage and Potatoes 182
    Candied Carrots 183
    Chinese Veggies and Rice 184
    Mom's Pennsylvania Dutch Chow-Chow 185
    Lisa's Crockpot Cheesy Corn and Peppers 186
    Lisa's Slow-Cooked Corn on the Cob 187
    Roasted Corn on the Cob 188
    Corn Pie 189
    Brenda's Baked Lima Beans 190
    Caramelized Onions 191
    Summer Squash Casserole 192
    Carolina Tomato Pie 193

Thanksgiving Favorites 195
    Brenda's Memories From Earlier Thanksgivings 196
    Brining Your Meats 197
    Corn Casserole 198
    Cranberry Relish 199
    Chuck and Wes' Deep-Fried Turkey 200
    Pennsylvania Dried Corn 202
    Westley Green Bean Casserole 203
    Jane Bleistine's Apricot Jell-O™ 204
    Oyster Stuffing 205
    Uncle Eddie's Pennsylvania Dutch Potato Filling 206
    Ed Gallagher's Sausage Cranberry Apple Stuffing 207
    Turkey Gravy 208

Desserts 209
    Grandma's Baking Tips 210
    Baking Flavor Enhancement Tips 214
    Amish Shoofly Pie 216
    French Apple Crisp 217
    Brenda's Glazed Apple Dumplings 218
    Tammy Bly's Blueberry Crumble 219
    Jane's Krispy Kreme™ Bread Pudding 220
    Joyce's Bread Pudding 221
    Cream Cheese Flan 222
    Classic Cheesecake 223
    Cherry Crescent Cheesecake Cups 225
    Grammie Jane's 4-Layer Cheesecake 226
    Lisa's Triple Rich Chocolate Cake 228
    Molten Chocolate Cake 229
    Deb and Jane's Crème Brûlée 230
    Crème Brûlée Bread Pudding 232
    Lisa and Lori's Enchanted Castle Cake 233

Fastnachts (Pennsylvania Dutch/German Yeast Doughnuts) 234
Wilson Fruit Cobbler 236
Key Lime Pie 237
Mom's Lemon Sponge Pie 239
Brenda's Mandarin Orange Cake 240
Grilled Peaches with Chocolate 241
Lisa's Peanut Butter Tandy Cake 242
Pie Crust 243
Pumpkin Pie 244
Festive Pumpkin Pie 245
Shana's Rhubarb Crumble 246
Brenda's Rice Pudding 247
Lisa's Sponge Cake 248
Joyce's Tapioca Pudding 249
Texas Sheet Cake 250

Cookies 251
Lisa's Banana Bars 252
Erica's Buckeyes 253
Salted Caramel Snickerdoodles 254
Aunt Marta's French Lace Cookies 255
Grammie Jane's Island Cookies 256
Homemade Nutter Butters™ 257
Oatmeal Chocolate Chip Cookies 258
Erica's Oreo™ Balls 259
Aunt Marta's No-Bake Peanut Butter Balls 260
Chocolate-Peanut Butter Candy Bars 261
Brenda's Sugar Cookies 262
Lisa's Whoopee Pies 263

Appendix: Conversion Chart 264

Appetizers

Deb's Asparagus-Prosciutto Rolls

Yields: 4 to 8 servings.

Ingredients:
- ¼ cup olive oil
- 1 Tablespoon red wine vinegar
- ½ Tablespoon Dijon mustard
- 1 clove garlic, crushed
- 1 Tablespoon minced fresh chives
- salt and pepper to taste
- 4 thin slices prosciutto, cut in half crosswise
- 3 Tablespoons cream cheese or goat cheese, divided
- 16 stalks asparagus with trimmed stems
- blanched Italian parsley for garnish

Directions:
1. Boil a pot of salted water and blanch the asparagus spears to a crispy tender state. Remove spears to an ice water bath to shock spears and pat spears dry. (Only take a couple of minutes so watch closely)
2. Combine the olive oil, vinegar, mustard, and garlic in a bowl; whisk well.
3. Stir in the chives and salt and pepper.
4. Spread each piece of prosciutto with ½ Tablespoon of cheese.
5. Roll 2 stalks of asparagus in each half of prosciutto.
6. Top with vinaigrette.

    Serve at room temperature.

Westley Bacon Wrapped Smokies

Ingredients

- 1 pound bacon, cut Into thirds
- 1 pound Lil' Smokies (small sausages)
- 1 stick butter
- 2 cups brown sugar

Directions:

1. Preheat oven to 375° F.
2. Cut the bacon into thirds and wrap each smokie (small sausage)
3. Coat baking dish with cooking oil spray and place all the wrapped smokies in a single layer in a baking dish.
4. Melt the stick of butter and 1 cup of brown sugar and stir until mixed well.
5. Pour the butter and brown sugar mixture on the smokies and bacon.
6. Then take the other cup of brown sugar and sprinkle evenly over the smokies.
7. Bake them for about 15-20 minutes and then turn the heat up to 400° F for about 5 minutes or longer until the bacon becomes crispy.
8. Cool, Transfer to serving dish and serve with toothpicks

Optional: add orange Juice and omit the butter

Chicken Liver Paté

Ingredients:
- 1 pound chicken livers
- 1 cup butter, melted
- ½ cup chopped sweet onion
- ¾ cup chopped stuffed green olives
- 1 teaspoon curry powder
- 1 teaspoon paprika
- ¼ teaspoon salt
- ¼ teaspoon pepper
- 4 Tablespoons brandy or cognac

Directions:
1. Melt ¼ cup of butter, add livers, onions, curry powder, salt, pepper, and paprika.
2. Cover and simmer for 10 to 15 minutes on medium-low heat
3. Blend cooked liver mixture in blender, adding brandy and remaining melted butter.
4. Pack mixture in small round bowl and refrigerate until firm
   Un-mold Paté on a serving plate and serve with cocktail rye bread and crackers.

Deb's Christmas Tree Roll-Ups

Ingredients:

    8-oz. package cream cheese, softened

    ½ cup chopped drained roasted red bell peppers (from 7¼-oz jar)

    ¼ cup chopped ripe olives

    ¼ cup chopped fresh basil leaves

    ¼ cup shredded Parmesan cheese

    4 spinach-flavor flour tortillas (8 to 10 inches in diameter)

    Ripe olive pieces

Directions:

1. In medium bowl, mix all ingredients except tortillas and olive pieces.
2. Divide mixture among tortillas, spreading to edges of tortillas.
3. Roll up tightly. Press each tortilla roll into triangle shape, using fingers. Wrap in plastic wrap. Refrigerate at least 2 hours but no longer than 24 hours.

To serve, cut rolls into ½-inch slices.

4. Place olive piece at bottom of each triangle to look like tree trunk; secure with toothpick.

If you don't have time to press this appetizer into the shape of Christmas trees, just prepare the filling as directed, spread on tortillas and roll up. Refrigerate 2 hours, and cut into slices.

This recipe is easy to cut in half for a smaller group.

Cocktail Bread Hors D'oeuvres

Ingredients:

    1 cup grated parmesan Cheese

    1 cup mayonnaise

    1 bunch scallions (use some green tops too), chopped

    Bacon (either crispy fried bacon crumbled or bacon bits)

    French bread baguettes or rye bread squares, about ⅛ inch thick slices

Directions:

1. Spread mayonnaise on bread slices
2. Sprinkle on cheese, scallions and bacon bits
3. Cook briefly under oven broiler till slightly brown

Serve and enjoy!

Deb's Coconut Shrimp

Ingredients

Dipping Sauce:

> ½ cup orange marmalade
>
> 4 teaspoons rice wine vinegar
>
> ½ teaspoon crushed red pepper flakes

Coconut Shrimp:

> Buy large size Shrimp preferably deveined and peeled (allow 3 to 4 shrimp per person)
>
> Peanut oil, for frying
>
> ½ cup all-purpose flour
>
> 1 teaspoon salt
>
> ½ teaspoon baking powder
>
> 1 can unsweetened coconut milk
>
> 2 cups shredded sweetened coconut
>
> ½ cup bread crumbs

Directions:

1. Add all dipping sauce ingredients to a pot on a low temperature. Heat for 10 minutes, making sure to stir ingredients every few minutes.
2. In a large, heavy pot, heat 2-inches of the peanut oil to 325* F.
3. Meanwhile, in a large bowl, whisk together the flour, salt, and baking powder.
4. Add the coconut milk and whisk until smooth. Let the batter stand for 15 minutes.
5. In a wide, shallow bowl, toss the coconut and bread crumbs together.
6. Put the shrimp into the batter. Remove the shrimp, 1 at a time, and dredge in the coconut mixture, pressing to help the coconut adhere.
7. Fry the shrimp in batches in the hot oil for 1 to 2 minutes or until brown. Use a slotted spoon to transfer the shrimp to a baking sheet lined with paper towels.

Serve the shrimp with the dipping sauce

Deb's Crab Bombs

Ingredients:

    1 lb. crabmeat

    1 egg, beaten

    1 cup Ritz™ crackers, crushed

    1 teaspoon yellow mustard

    2 Tablespoons fresh lemon Juice

    2 Tablespoons fresh parsley, chopped

    1 teaspoon Old Bay™ seasoning

    1 Tablespoon Worcestershire sauce

Directions:

1. Place crabmeat in a mixing bowl, picking out any stray shell fragments.
2. Add crushed crackers, Old Bay™ seasoning and parsley to the crab.
3. In a separate bowl, combine egg, mustard, lemon juice and Worcestershire sauce. Whip with a whisk until smooth.
4. Pour egg mixture over the crabmeat and crackers and gently mix careful not to break up large lumps of crabmeat.
5. Mold into golf ball sized balls and place on a cookie sheet.
6. Bake at 350° F for 30 minutes.
7. Drizzle with melted butter and allow to cool.

Westley Deviled Eggs

Servings: 12 to 18

Ingredients:

- 12 large eggs
- ¼ cup mayonnaise or creamy Caesar dressing
- 3 pickled gherkins, minced or sweet relish
- 2 teaspoons Dijon mustard
- 1½ teaspoons minced shallot or minced sweet onion
- 2 teaspoons snipped chives
- Kosher salt and freshly ground pepper, sweet paprika
- 4 ounces your choice of thinly sliced country ham, prosciutto, or cooked bacon torn or chopped into pieces.
- ½ cup shredded Parmesan cheese

Directions:

1. In a large saucepan, cover the eggs with cold water and bring to a boil over high heat. Boil for 5 minutes, then turn the heat off and let the eggs stand in the hot water for 10 minutes. Transfer the eggs to an ice water bath until chilled, about 5 minutes. Peel the eggs and halve them lengthwise. Set the egg whites on a serving platter.

2. In a medium bowl, mash the yolks, and mix in the gherkins/relish, mustard, shallot/onion. Add half the chive and ham/bacon into the mixture.

3. Add and adjust the amount of mayonnaise so the mixture becomes smooth and firm but not sloppy. Season with salt and pepper.

4. Add the egg yolk mixture into a zip lock bag and cut a corner off the bag in order to pipe the filling into the egg white halves; (as an alternate, use a spoon to fill the egg white halves.)

5. Top each egg with your selection of pieces of chopped country ham/prosciutto/bacon and chives,

6. Sprinkle with Parmesan cheese & paprika and serve.

Westley Pickled Eggs and Beets

Makes great Pennsylvania Red Beet Eggs found in Old Dutch Bar Taverns.

Ingredients:

- 2 cans/jars (15 ounces each) whole/quartered pickled beets
- 12 fresh eggs
- 1 cup sugar
- 1 cup water
- 1 cup cider vinegar

Directions:

1. In a large saucepan, cover the eggs with cold water and bring to a boil over high heat. Remove from the heat and let the eggs stand in the hot water for 10 minutes. Transfer the eggs to an ice water bath until chilled, about 5 minutes. Peel eggs
2. Drain beets, reserving 1cup juice (discard remaining juice or save for another use). Cup beets into nice serving sizes
3. Layer cut beets and peeled eggs in a 2-qt. glass jar or a couple of 1-qt. canning jars
4. In a small saucepan, bring the sugar, water, vinegar and re served beet juice to a boil
5. Pour over beets and eggs; let cool
6. Cover tightly and refrigerate for at least 24 hours before serving.

Westley Scallion Cheese Roll-Ups

Ingredients:

    1 pound thinly-sliced dried beef or your favorite lunchmeat slices like Maple Honey Ham

    8 oz. soft cream cheese with chives

    8 oz. Boursin cheese

    3 - 4 bunches scallions or spring onions

Directions:

1. Clean and trim scallions to about 4 inches in length. (You may want to save the green tops for a garnish or for other dip recipes.)
2. Mix cream and Boursin cheeses together. A quick 15-second warm-up in the microwave helps with the mixing.
3. Lay a spring onion on the side of a piece of dried beef.
4. Spread cheese mixture along the length of the spring onion.
5. Roll the dried beef, spring onion and cheese into a cylinder.

    Place on a serving platter.

Indian Kebobs

Ingredients:

- 1 block *paneer*
- 1 cup plain yogurt
- 2 Tablespoons *tandoori masala*
- 1 Tablespoon red chili powder
- 2 - 3 cloves fresh crushed garlic
- 1 Tablespoon *garam masala*
- salt to taste

Directions:

1. Cut *paneer* in cubes
2. Mix remaining ingredients and add the *paneer* cubes
3. Let marinate in the fridge for 3 - 4 hours
4. Once you are ready to cook, just mix other veggies in the same sauce for a few minutes and you are ready to grill

Shana's PA Dutch Soft Pretzels

Preparation time: 1 hour
Total time: 2½ hours
Makes: 12 pretzels

Ingredients:

Dough Prep:

⅓ cup baking soda

3 cups flour

2¼ teaspoons or 1 package instant yeast

3 Tablespoons dark brown sugar

½ teaspoon salt

⅛ teaspoon pepper

2 Tablespoons room temperature butter, cut in 8 pieces

1 cup warm water

Cooking:

8 cups water (2 quarts)

1 Tablespoon brown sugar

1 egg yolk, beaten with 1 Tablespoon water

Coarse salt for sprinkling

continued on next page

continued from previous page

Directions:

1. Preheat oven to 250° F. Spread baking soda on baking sheet and bake for 30 minutes. Set aside to cool.

2. In a large bowl, whisk together flour, yeast, brown sugar, salt and pepper. Stir in butter, then make a well in the center and add the water slowly. Mix until the dough comes together in a shaggy mass. Using your hands, gather dough and turn out onto a lightly floured surface. Knead for several minutes until it is no longer sticky. Cover with plastic, and let rise in a warm place for 30 minutes.

3. Turn dough out onto your work surface and cut into 12 equal pieces. Roll each piece into an 18-inch rope and set aside. If the dough seems sticky, flour your hands (not the counter) and roll. Repeat with remaining pieces.

4. Place parchment paper on 2 baking pans and generously spray with cooking or baking oil.

5. Preheat oven to 425 degrees, and place racks on bottom and upper third of oven.

6. With each rope of dough, form a U shape and make a twist about 3 inches from the ends. Fold the twisted portion backward along center of U to form a pretzel shape, then gently press ends onto the dough to seal. Transfer to the baking sheet. After all are shaped, cover each pan with a clean towel and let rest for 20 minutes.

7. While the pretzels are resting, bring 2 quarts of water to a boil, and then add brown sugar, and the baking soda. This combination will froth. Stir to dissolve, and then reduce heat to a simmer.

8. Carefully place three pretzels at a time, topside down, into the water. After 30 seconds, turn pretzels over. After another 30 seconds, lift with a slotted spoon or spatula, tapping to shed excess water, and return to oiled parchment paper. Repeat with remaining pretzels.

9. Brush each pretzel with egg yolk mixture, trying to drip as little as possible onto the parchment, then sprinkle with coarse salt.

10. Bake for 7 minutes, then switch pan positions on racks and bake for another 7 minutes.

11. Transfer pretzels to wire racks to cool. Serve immediately, or keep uncovered at room temperature for up to 12 hours.

    Rewarm in a 250° F oven, if desired.

Notes:
- These are best eaten on the same day as baked. Pretzels can be frozen for up to one month.
- The dough may be mixed the night before and refrigerated but remove dough from refrigerator at least 30 minutes before shaping pretzels.

Zack Pirtle's Spicy Hot Popcorn

Cooking popcorn with your own popcorn machine at home is a great and healthy snack. After making the popcorn, I put a light mixing of sriracha sauce on top, mixing the popcorn as I go so that a small amount of sauce gets mixed onto most of the pieces of popcorn. Top lightly with salt.

Ingredients:

    Sriracha sauce

    Popcorn machine: cooking in pot can be done with training.

    Popcorn kernels: I usually buy a large container.

    Salt

Variations:

    You can add olive oil to the popcorn kernels as you cook it, to simulate butter. If you do want to add butter, you can melt the butter in the microwave and add it on.

Westley Trail Mix

Our go-to snack mix
I don't even miss the butter, soy sauce, etc. in the
original ChexMix™ recipe.

Ingredients:

- ¾ cup roasted peanuts
- ½ cup raisins
- 1¼ cups crispy whole-wheat cereal square
- 1¼ cups crispy rice squares
- 1 cup mini pretzels
- ½ cup chocolate chips or M&M™'s

Directions:

1. In a large bowl, coming all ingredients
2. Place in an air-tight container or zip-lock plastic bag
3. Store in a cool, dry place

Chef's Notes:

- Use any of your favorite nuts or dried fruits in place of the peanuts and raisins. I prefer dried cherries.
- Use any whole grain, low-sugar cereal instead of the crispy whole-wheat cereal squares. I even use Cheerios™.
- This snack is high in protein, iron, and fiber. However, it can also be high in calories depending on what ingredients you use.

Lisa's Cool Veggie Pizza

Ingredients:

    1 can refrigerator crescent rolls

    2 8-oz. packages cream cheese

    1½ Tablespoons mayonnaise

    Dill weed

    Favorite vegetables (zucchini, mushrooms, green peppers, onions, tomatoes, cucumbers, etc.)

Directions:

1. Spread crescent roll dough on pizza sheet or cookie sheet.
2. Bake at 350° F until lightly brown.
3. Remove from oven and let cool completely.
4. Blend together softened cream cheese, mayonnaise, and dill weed.
5. Spread the cheese mixture on top of cold crust.
6. Finely chop veggies (zucchini, mushrooms, green peppers, green onions, tomatoes, cucumbers, etc.
7. Sprinkle a layer of each vegetable over cheese layer,
8. Chill before serving

Beverages

Brandy Alexander

Ingredients:

    1½ cups brandy

    1 cup *Crème De Cacao*

    1 cup half-and-half

    2 scoops vanilla ice cream

    2 cups ice

    Nutmeg

Directions:

1. In a blender, add first 5 ingredients and blend until the consistency of a milk shake.
2. Serve in a stem glass and add a dusting of nutmeg on top

Cranberry Drink Garnish

Excellent as an addition to cranberry drinks, or as a garnish on ice cream.

Ingredients:

    5½ oz. cranberries

    2 cups water

    ¾ cup sugar

    2 teaspoons freshly graded lime zest

Directions:

1. Combine first 3 ingredients and bring to high heat until berries pop, then turn down to simmer
2. Pulverize cranberries to a mash
3. Strain berry mixture
4. Pour onto flat cookie sheet
5. Put in freezer to set
6. Add lime zest
7. Scrape cranberry ice into shaved crystals

Ed Sr.'s Bourbon Eggnog

Ed Sr. was renown for making and serving his Eggnog drink during the Christmas holidays.

His Bourbon Eggnog recipe will show you just how easy and delicious eggnog can be and you can use it to keep the Gallagher holiday tradition alive. The origins of eggnog can be traced back to the 17th century and it has been a Christmas favorite ever since.

Eggnog is best with good bourbon. The flavors of the bourbon pair well with the holiday spices. This recipe also features a little brandy and orange liqueur to create even more dimensions of flavor. It is extremely easy to make and is far better than any prepared eggnog found at the store. It is delicious and is a great way to impress family and friends during the holiday season.

It is strongly recommended to make this eggnog a day before you need it. The extra time allows all of the tastes to marry and become one delicious and impressive drink.

Yield: about 8 4-ounce servings

Ingredients:
- 4 large eggs
- 6 ounces sugar (granulated)
- 1 teaspoon nutmeg (freshly grated)
- ⅛ teaspoon allspice
- ⅛ teaspoon clove
- ½ teaspoon cinnamon
- 2 ounces Cognac
- 2 ounces Grand Marnier (a vanilla liqueur can be substituted here as well)
- 4 ounces Bourbon
- 12 ounces whole milk
- 8 ounces heavy cream

Directions:
1. Blend the eggs for 1 minute in either a mixer or a blender.
2. Add the sugar and spices and blend for an additional 30 seconds to incorporate.
3. Slowly add the liquors and blend another 30 seconds.
4. Add the milk and cream and blend 1 minute more.
5. Cover and refrigerate.

Serving:
- Portion out 4 ounces of eggnog into a champagne flute or teacup.
- Grate fresh nutmeg or cinnamon over the top (optional).
- Serve and enjoy!

Slow-Cooked Hot Chocolate

Prep Time: 25 minutes
Servings: 8 - 10

Use your crock-pot or slow cooker to make the easiest hot chocolate ever, then top mugs with pre-made frozen dollops of whipped cream.

Ingredients:

Hot Chocolate:

1 pound semi-sweet chocolate chips

2 quarts whole milk

2 cups heavy cream

14-ounce can sweetened condensed milk

½ teaspoon pure vanilla extract

½ teaspoon kosher salt

Frozen Whipped Cream:

2 cups heavy cream

¼ cup confectioners' sugar

½ teaspoon pure vanilla extract

Directions:

Slow-Cooker Hot Chocolate:

1. Combine all ingredients in a 6-quart slow cooker and mix well.

2. Cook on low for 2 hours, stirring occasionally.

3. Ladle the hot chocolate into mugs, top with frozen whipped cream dollops and serve.

Frozen Whipped Cream:

1. In a large bowl, using a hand mixer, beat the heavy cream with the sugar and vanilla at medium-high speed until smooth and thick.

2. Decoratively dollop the whipped cream on a foil-lined baking sheet and freeze until firm, about 2 hours.

3. Using a small offset spatula, transfer the dollops onto mugs of hot chocolate and serve.

Spring Lemonade

Yield: 3 quarts

Ingredients:

    6 cups white grape juice, chilled

    12-ounce can frozen lemonade concentrate, thawed and undiluted

    5½ cups club soda, chilled

Directions:

1. Stir together all ingredients in a 1-gallon pitcher or punch bowl.
2. Serve over ice.

Southern Sweet Tea

Ingredients:

    Simple Syrup:

        2 cups sugar (Don't worry - not all of that goes in the tea!)
        2 cups water

    Tea:

        4 cups water
        8 - 10 regular-sized or 3 "family sized" orange pekoe tea bags
        Pinch of baking soda
        Additional water as needed

Directions:

    Simple Syrup:

1. Pour water and sugar into a saucepan and stir.
2. Bring to a boil, reduce heat, and stir until thickened.
3. Turn off heat, and set aside to cool
4. Pour into glass canning jars and cover to use in numerous Tea preparations.

    Tea:

1. Strip tags from the tea bags, and tie strings to the handle of a wooden spoon, near the bowl.
2. Bring water to a boil in a saucepan. Turn off the heat, and place the tea-tied wooden spoon in the pan with a pinch of baking soda (It smooths out the tea's tannins.).
3. Once it has suitably darkened and is still hot, pull out the spoon. (Refrain from squeezing the teabags, as that clouds the tea.)
4. Stir 1 cup of the sugar syrup into the tea until it's thoroughly blended.
5. Pour the mixture into a 1 gallon glass or metal pitcher and fill to the top with water.
6. Stir and chill in the refrigerator.
7. Once the tea has cooled, serve it in tall glasses ⅔-filled with ice.
8. Serve with sugar syrup on the side so that guests may sweeten according to their personal taste.

Y'all come back now, hear?

Dips

Seven Layer Refried Bean Dip

Ingredients:

- 1-ounce package taco seasoning mix
- 16-ounce can refried beans
- 8-ounce package cream cheese, softened
- 16-ounce container sour cream
- 16-ounce jar salsa
- 1 large tomato, chopped
- 1 green bell pepper, chopped
- 1 bunch chopped scallions or green onions
- 1 small head iceberg lettuce, shredded
- 6-ounce can sliced black olives, drained
- 2 cups Cheddar cheese, shredded

Directions:

1. In a medium bowl, blend the taco seasoning mix and refried beans. Spread the mixture onto a large serving platter.
2. Mix the sour cream and cream cheese in a medium bowl. Spread over the re fried beans.
3. Top the layers with salsa.
4. Place a layer of tomato, green bell pepper, green onions and lettuce over the salsa
5. Top with Cheddar cheese. Garnish with black olives.

Serve with your favorite selection of strong dipping chips and/or crackers.

Deb's Clam Dip

Ingredients:

    2 6-ounce cans minced clams (1 drained, 1 not drained)

    1 stick sweet butter, melted

    2 sleeves Ritz™ crackers, 1 crumbled, 1 not

    1 small white onion, finely chopped

    2 cloves garlic, minced (1 Tablespoon)

    ¼ cup grated Parmesan cheese

Directions:

1. Preheat oven to 350° F.
2. Drain one can of clams and place into a large mixing bowl. Add the second can of clams with the liquid.
3. Mix in the crumbled crackers. Add the butter, onion, garlic and Parmesan cheese and combine.
4. Put mixture into an onion soup crock. Bake for 30 minutes until golden brown.
5. Let stand for 5 to 10 minutes before serving.

Serve with Ritz™ crackers and a spreading knife.

Crab Imperial with Red Pepper

Crab imperial is a classic Maryland dish made with blue crab bound in a mayonnaise-based sauce. Here we make a hollandaise sauce instead, which makes the spread even silkier.

Total Time: 40 minutes
Servings: 8 First-Course Servings

Ingredients:

- 1 stick unsalted butter: 6 Tablespoons melted, the remainder for greasing
- 2 Tablespoons all-purpose flour
- 1½ cups milk
- Salt
- Freshly ground pepper
- 1 Tablespoon extra-virgin olive oil
- 1 small sweet onion, finely diced
- ½ red bell pepper, cut into ¼-inch cubes
- 2 large egg yolks
- 2 Tablespoons fresh lemon juice
- Finely grated zest of 1 lemon
- Hot sauce, such as Crystal™ or Tabasco™
- 1 pound lump crabmeat, picked over
- Toasted baguette slices for serving

Directions:

1. In a saucepan, melt 2 Tablespoons of the butter over moderate heat. Stir in the flour to make a paste. Gradually whisk in the milk until smooth and the sauce thickens.

2. Reduce the heat to low and cook, whisking, until no floury taste remains, about 7 minutes. Season with salt and pepper. Cover and remove from the heat.

3. In a skillet, heat the oil. Add the bell pepper and cook over moderate heat until softened, add the onion and cook until translucent. Season with salt and pepper.

4. In a stainless steel bowl, whisk the egg yolks with the lemon juice. Set the bowl over (not in) a saucepan of simmering water and whisk constantly until thickened, approx. 2 minutes;

5. Remove the egg yolk mixture from the heat and slowly whisk in the 6 Tablespoons melted butter until a smooth sauce forms. Fold in the flour paste and lemon zest. Season with salt, pepper and hot sauce.

6. Preheat the broiler. Set one rack 6 inches from the heat and another rack 10 inches below the top rack. Butter a 9-by-9-inch ceramic baking dish.

7. In a bowl, combine the crabmeat, onion and bell pepper. Gently fold in the sauce. Scrape into the prepared baking dish.

8. Broil on the upper rack for 3 minutes, until browned. Transfer the baking dish to the lower rack and broil for 4 minutes longer, until hot throughout.

Serve with baguette toasts.

Cream Cheese Dip

Ingredients:
- 16 oz. Philadelphia™ cream cheese
- 8 oz. Boursin cheese blend
- 6 oz. sliced Honey Maple ham lunchmeat, chopped
- 6 Tablespoons chopped scallions - both white and green parts

Directions:
1. Add cheeses to a microwave-safe serving dip bowl.
2. Microwave cheeses until they are soft for mixing. (approx. 30 seconds)
3. Add chopped ham and scallions.
4. Mix well

Serve with favorite crackers

Whipped Lemon Ricotta Dip

Easily turns a container of average grocery store ricotta into a creamy and elegant whipped lemon ricotta dip to serve with crackers.

Prep Time: 10 minutes
Yield: 2 cups

Ingredients:

- 2 cups whole-milk ricotta cheese
- ¼ cup heavy cream
- 1 lemon, zested
- Optional toppings: flaky sea salt, freshly ground black pepper, olive oil, chili flakes
- Baguettes or crackers for serving

Directions:

1. Combine ricotta, heavy cream, and lemon zest in the bowl of an electric stand mixer. Whip 5 minutes, or until ricotta is light and fluffy.
2. Transfer into a serving bowl and garnish with desired toppings (drizzle of oil, sprinkle of salt and/or pepper, etc.)

Serve with bread or crackers on the side.

Mexican Dip

Ingredients:

    1 12-ounce roll of Jimmy Dean™ or Jones™ sausage

    1 brick Mexican Velveeta™ or regular Velveeta™ cheese with 2 to 3 Tablespoons canned chopped green chilies on the side

    1 bag Doritos™

Directions:

1. Preheat oven to 350° F.
2. Cut the Velveeta™ into cubes and melt in microwave for 2 minutes or put cheese into a double boiler over medium high heat and melt. This takes about 10 minutes.
3. In a large frying pan, cook the sausage over medium high heat breaking it into small bits as it browns. This takes 15 minutes until it is golden brown.
4. Drain the sausage on paper towels. Add the sausage to the melted cheese (if using regular Velveeta™ add the chopped chilies.)
5. Place into a 10-inch oval baking dish.
6. Bake in pre-heated oven for 20 minutes. Let stand 5 to 10 minutes before serving.

Serve while hot with Doritos™ for dipping.

Roasted Onion Dip

Prep Time: 45 minutes
Total Time: 2 hours 45 minutes
Servings: 10 to 12

Ingredients:

    2 medium unpeeled red onions

    2 medium unpeeled Spanish onions

    2 medium unpeeled sweet onions

    ½ cup mayonnaise

    ½ cup sour cream

    ½ teaspoon onion powder

    Kosher salt

    Pepper

    Fennel fronds, as a garnish

    Salmon, trout, and sturgeon caviar, for serving

    Herbed potato chips, for serving

Directions:

1. Preheat the oven to 350° F. Using a paring knife, trim the bottoms of the onions and stand them in a baking dish. Bake for about 1 hour and 30 minutes, until very soft. Let cool.

2. Using a paring knife, carefully cut ½ inch off the top of the onions. Using a small spoon, scoop out all but 2 or 3 layers of the roasted onions to form cups; you should have 2½ cups of pulp.

3. Finely chop the onion pulp and transfer to a medium bowl. Stir in the mayonnaise, sour cream and onion powder and season the dip generously with salt and pepper. Cover and refrigerate until chilled, about 30 minutes.

4. Keep the onion cups at room temperature. Spoon the onion dip into the onion cups and transfer to a platter. Top the dip with salmon, trout, and sturgeon caviar and garnish with fennel fronds.

    Serve with herbed potato chips.

To Make Ahead:

    The onion cups and onion dip can be refrigerated separately overnight. Let the onion cups return to room temperature before filling them.

Vidalia Onion Dip

Ingredients:

    3 Vidalia onions chopped

    3 cups shredded Swiss cheese

    1 cup mayonnaise

    1 to 3 teaspoons minced garlic

Directions:

1. Preheat oven to 350* F.
2. Grease casserole dish
3. Mix ingredients and add to dish
4. Bake 35 to 40 minutes until bubbly

    Serve with Fritos™ or Tortilla Chips

Supreme Pizza Dip

Ingredients:

- 1 8-ounce block cream cheese, room temperature
- ¼ teaspoon dried oregano
- ¼ teaspoon dried basil
- ¼ teaspoon red pepper flakes
- ¼ teaspoon garlic powder
- 1 cup mozzarella cheese, shredded
- 1 cup pizza sauce
- ½ cup Cheddar cheese, shredded
- ½ cup Parmesan cheese, shredded
- ¼ cup ground Italian sausage, cooked
- 10 slices pepperoni
- 3 Tablespoons green bell pepper, diced
- 3 Tablespoons black olives, sliced
- ¼ cup mushrooms, sliced

Directions:

1. Preheat oven to 350° F.
2. In a medium bowl, mix together cream cheese and spices.
3. Spread mixture into the bottom of an oven safe 9-inch deep dish pie plate.
4. Top cream cheese mixture with ½ cup mozzarella and spread pizza sauce over it.
5. Sprinkle the remaining cheese over the sauce and top with sausage, pepperoni, bell pepper, olives and mushrooms.
6. Bake for 15 - 20 minutes or until the cheese is golden brown and bubbly.

   Serve immediately with garlic toast or baguettes and enjoy!

Blue Cheese Dip

Ingredients::

- 1 8-oz. container marscapone cheese (can substitute cream cheese if unavailable)
- 1 cup sour cream
- ¼ cup diced green onions (3 - 4)
- 8 oz. crumbled Gorgonzola cheese
- ½ teaspoon salt
- ½ teaspoon pepper

Directions:

1. Mix together soft cheese
2. Add salt, pepper, sour cream, and green onions. Stir well
3. Add Gorgonzola cheese and stir.

    It is best to make it the night before, but at least 4 hours before serving so the flavors blend. Serve with crackers, baguette, sliced apples, pears. Enjoy!!!

Breakfasts

Brenda's Baked Oatmeal

I developed this recipe from the version served at Pansy Hill, a local Lebanon, PA restaurant. It's a "healthy" version with very little sugar and fat. You definitely need to add sugar or sweetener to it in the bowl, or you could add it right in to the recipe. I think it came out a little less dense than the Pansy Hill version — maybe that's a good thing. The "traditional" recipes call for 4 Tablespoons butter instead of the teaspoon of oil, less milk (1 cup), and replace the applesauce with brown sugar.

Makes 8 servings

Ingredients:

- 2 cups regular or quick-cooking oats
- 1½ teaspoon baking powder
- 1 teaspoon ground cinnamon
- 2 Tablespoons dark brown sugar (I use the Splenda™ Brown Sugar Blend instead)
- ⅓ cup chopped pecans
- 1 egg
- 1 egg white
- 1½ cups skim milk
- 1 teaspoon vanilla extract
- 1 teaspoon vegetable oil
- ½ cup no-sugar-added apple sauce
- Cooking spray

Directions:

1. Preheat oven to 350° F degrees.
2. Combine oats, baking powder, cinnamon, dark brown sugar and chopped pecans in a large bowl and mix to blend.
3. Beat egg and egg white in a medium bowl and then add milk, vanilla, vegetable oil and apple sauce.
4. Add milk mixture to oat mixture and stir well.
5. Spray a 9-inch pie pan with cooking spray. Pour oat mixture into pie pan a
6. Bake in the oven for 35 - 40 minutes or until toothpick inserted into the center comes out clean.

Joyce's Creamed Dried Beef

As Joyce would say, "This is an extremely easy and forgiving recipe. Use your common sense to adjust the recipe for the size and number of skillets you need for the number of hungry Dutchmen you have waiting for breakfast."

Serves approximately 4 hungry Pennsylvania Dutchmen

Ingredients:

- 2 lbs original Lebanon dried beef (imported from Lebanon, PA), sliced
- 1 large sweet onion
- ½ lb butter
- 4 heaping Tablespoons flour
- Milk
- Bread, muffins, or waffles
- Note: avoid adding salt as the dried beef is cured with salt

Directions

1. Put your largest frying skillet on medium high heat
2. Dice onion into small pieces
3. Sauté diced onion in four Tablespoons of butter until translucent and set aside
4. Cut or tear dried beef into bite sized pieces
5. Melt the rest of the butter in the skillet and add shredded dried beef
6. Fry dried beef until it browns
7. Sprinkle flour over dried beef, stir, and cook until flour browns
8. Add milk to cover dried beef mixture in skillet
9. Stir in sautéed onions or serve them on the side, depending on your guests' preferences.
10. Stir mixture occasionally while toasting your preferred "shingles" or pieces of bread
11. Remove from heat after mixture reaches your desired consistency

    Ladle generously over toasted shingle and *bon appétit!!!*

Hearty Egg Burritos

Serves 4

Ingredients:

- 3 green onions
- 1 medium red or green bell pepper
- 1 medium clove garlic
- 2 ounces low fat cheddar cheese, grated
- 15½ oz. can black beans
- 1 teaspoon canola oil
- 4 large eggs
- 1 teaspoon ground cumin, divided
- ¾ teaspoon ground black pepper
- Cooking spray or oil
- 4 8-inch whole wheat flour tortillas

Optional Ingredients:

- ⅓ cup nonfat plain yogurt
- ¼ cup fresh cilantro, rinsed and chopped

Directions:

1. Rinse green onions and bell pepper, Peel garlic glove.
2. Slice green onions, Remove core and seeds and dice bell pepper. Mince garlic
3. In a colander, drain and rinse beans
4. In a medium skillet over medium heat, heat oil. Add beans, green onions, bell pepper and garlic. Cook until peppers are soft, about 3 minutes. Add ¾ teaspoon ground cumin and black pepper. Transfer mixture to a plate
5. In a small bowl, crack eggs. Add remaining ¼ teaspoon cumin. Beat mixture lightly with a fork
6. Wipe out skillet with a paper towel. Coat with oil and heat at medium low. Add egg mixture. Cook, stirring occasionally, until eggs are as firm as you like - about 3 to 5 minutes. If using cilantro, add now
7. Spoon egg mixture into the center of each tortilla, dividing evenly. Add beans and veggies. Sprinkle cheese on top. If using yogurt, add a dollop to each tortilla.
8. Add mixture, fold and serve.

Note: Add color and flavor with a fresh salsa: mix chopped fresh or canned tomatoes, chopped onion and chopped cilantro, and add a pinch of ground cumin for heat. For a different flavor use a different cheese.

Wes' Egg Rollups

Flexible for meat eaters and vegetarians alike.
Adjust quantities for number of hungry Dutchmen

Ingredients:

    Eggs

    Select a main meat or vegetable: sausage, bacon, ham, or a combination

    Select a favorite cheese: cheddar, Swiss, Muenster, or a combination

    Sweet onion, & sweet red pepper

    Butter

    Sour cream

Directions:

1. Dice and sauté the onion and red pepper until soft. Set aside
2. Cook select meat or vegetables and cut/crumble into small pieces. Set aside
3. Grate your cheese selection
4. Break two eggs into bowl; add favorite seasonings & herbs, beat for uniform consistency
5. Preheat 8-inch fry pan and coat with butter on medium heat
6. Add egg mixture to uniformly coat bottom of fry pan
7. Add a strip of grated cheese diagonally across the omelet
8. Add a sprinkling of crumbled meat or vegetables over strip of cheese
9. Add a sprinkling of sautéed onion and red pepper over strip of cheese
10. Cook until the egg's surface sets and omelet gentle slides in fry pan (placing a pot lid over the cooking egg mixture will help the eggs cook without burning)
11. Add dash of sour cream over top of diagonal strip
12. Use a fork to fold the two edge halves of cooked egg over the center strip
13. Gently slide egg rollup onto serving dish

    Hold cooked rollups in warn oven for a group breakfast serving.

Jane's Bananas Foster French Toast

Makes 8 servings

Ingredients:

- 1 stick plus 2 Tablespoons butter
- 1 cup pecan pieces
- 2 cups maple syrup
- ¼ cup rum
- 3 eggs
- ¾ cup milk
- 1 Tablespoon grated orange zest
- ¼ cup fresh orange juice
- 2 Tablespoons sugar
- ¼ teaspoon cinnamon
- ¼ teaspoon vanilla extract
- 8 slices French bread, about 1 inch thick
- 2 bananas, peeled and sliced, ¼ inch thick
- powdered sugar for dusting

Directions:

1. In a sauté pan, melt 2 Tablespoons of the butter.
2. Add the pecans and sauté for 4 - 5 minutes, stirring constantly.
3. Stir in the maple syrup and bring the liquid up to a simmer.
4. Remove the pan from the stove and add the rum. Carefully place the pan back on the stove and flame the sauce. Remove the sauce from the heat and set aside.
5. In a mixing bowl whisk the eggs, milk, orange zest, orange juice, sugar, cinnamon, and vanilla, to dissolve the sugar.
6. In a nonstick sauté pan heat 2 Tablespoons butter. Dip 2 slices of the bread into the egg-milk mixture, coating evenly. Fry in the butter until golden brown, 2-3 minutes on each side. Repeat until all the butter and bread are used.
7. Lay the french toast on a platter.
8. Add the bananas to the pecan mixture and warm slightly. Spoon the warm sauce over the French toast. Dust the entire plate with powdered sugar.

Lisa's Baked French Toast

Ingredients:

- 1 *baguette* French bread, cut into 1" thick slices
- 6 large eggs
- 1½ cups milk
- 1 cup half and half
- 1 teaspoon vanilla
- ¼ teaspoon cinnamon
- ¼ teaspoon nutmeg
- ¼ cup butter or margarine, softened
- ½ cup light brown sugar
- ½ cup walnuts, chopped
- 1 Tablespoon light corn syrup

Directions:

1. The night before, butter a 9" square baking dish. Arrange bread slices, overlapping to fill dish completely.
2. Combine eggs, milk, half & half, vanilla, cinnamon and nutmeg. Mix well, then poor over bread slices.
3. Cover and refrigerate overnight.
4. The next day, preheat oven to 350° F.
5. Combine butter with brown sugar, walnuts, and corn syrup. Mix well, then spread evenly over soaked bread in pan.
6. Bake 40 minutes or until done.

Waffle Hash Browns

Ingredients:

    Olive oil cooking spray

    1 30-ounce bag frozen shredded hash browns, thawed

    4 Tablespoons (½ stick) butter, melted

    1 teaspoon kosher salt

    ½ teaspoon freshly ground black pepper

    ¾ cup grated cheddar cheese

    ¾ cup chopped ham

Directions:

1. Preheat a waffle iron on the regular setting and spray both sides with cooking spray.
2. Squeeze out any excess moisture from the hash browns and put in a bowl. Pour the melted butter over the hash browns, sprinkle with the salt and pepper and stir.
3. Scoop a heaping ½-cup of the seasoned hash browns into each waffle section, and then top with a generous 2 Tablespoons Cheddar followed by a sprinkling of chopped ham.
4. Top the cheese and ham in each section with another ¼-cup hash browns.
5. Close the waffle iron and cook for 15 minutes on the regular setting.
6. Repeat with the remaining hash browns, cheese and ham.

Potato Chip Omelet

Ingredients:

    12 large eggs

    12 ounces salted potato chips (preferably kettle-cooked style)

    1 large sweet onion

    Olive or vegetable oil, for cooking

Directions:

1. Preheat oven to 350° F.
2. In a large bowl, crack and whisk the eggs. Add the potato chips and toss well to coat, and set aside.
3. Heat 2 Tablespoons of oil in an ovenproof (preferably nonstick) 10 - 12-inch skillet with 2-inch sides over medium-high heat. Add the onions and sauté just until translucent.
4. Add the egg and potato chip mixture and let cook, stirring slightly to distribute onions and potato chips.
5. Transfer to oven and bake about 30 minutes, or until eggs are slightly puffed on edges and fully set in the center.

    Remove from oven. Slice and serve immediately.

Grandma's Tips for Making Light and Fluffy Pancakes

Mix dry ingredients (flours, baking soda, salt, sugar) in one bowl. **Mix wet ingredients** in another bowl. Then **stir the two together gently and evenly**, but do not over mix or the pancakes will be tough.

Separate the eggs (yolks and whites). Mix the yolks with the wet ingredients. Whip the egg whites until peaks form. Gently fold the whites into the final batter.

Let the batter rest about 30 minutes to 1 hour before making pancakes. For fluffy pancakes, the batter should be thick. (But don't let it rest too long or the batter will become too thick and you will need to thin it with a liquid before using.) Resting time allows the gluten to relax and it also allows the flour to absorb the liquid. **Give the batter a stir before using.**

Preheat a griddle to 375° F. Or use a heavy-bottom skillet. Use a small amount of oil or shortening to grease the griddle. Pour batter in ¼ cupfuls onto the hot skillet. Cook about 3 minutes or until you see bubbles forming on top and the edges are dry. Flip and cook another 2 minutes on the other side.

For a group breakfast, hold cooked pancakes in a 200° F oven to keep warm.

Orange Oatmeal Pancakes

Ingredients:

- ½ cup all-purpose flour
- ½ cup whole-wheat flour
- ½ cup quick oats
- 1 Tablespoon baking powder
- ¼ teaspoon salt
- 1 large egg
- ¾ cup orange juice
- ½ cup milk
- 2 Tablespoons canola oil

Directions:

1. In a large bowl, combine flours, oats, baking powder and salt. Mix well.
2. In another large bowl, crack egg, beat lightly with a fork
3. Add orange juice, milk and canola oil to egg. Mix well
4. Coat large skillet with oil or cooking spray. Heat over medium-high heat
5. Add wet ingredients to dry ingredients. Stir just until dry ingredients are moistened. Do not over mix.
6. Pour ¼ cup batter into hot pan for each pancake. Adjust heat as needed to avoid burning
7. Flip pancakes when bubbles appear on top of the batter and the edges are slightly browned, about 3 to 4 minutes. Cook until second side is slightly browned, about 2 to 3 minutes

    Serve warm

Chef Notes:

- Make a double batch, cook, and then freeze the cooked leftovers. To prevent the pancakes from sticking together, layer with waxed paper.
- Warm pancakes in a microwave or toaster oven for a quick breakfast.
- Top with berries, sliced banana, or maple syrup.
- If you are not a whole-wheat flour fan, use 1 cup all-purpose flour and omit the whole-wheat flour.

Esther Gallagher's Baked Pineapple Casserole

This is a Lancaster County dish. I was always amazed that the Lebanon relatives never had this dish, as Lebanon County is right next door. Oh well, leave it up to an Erie City girl to introduce this dish to the family.

This is a good side dish to accompany baked ham. It's good served hot or cold. Leftovers are always good served cold with milk or whipped cream poured over it! Enjoy!!

Serves 6 to 8

Ingredients:

½ cup butter, softened

1 cup sugar

4 eggs

5 - 7 slices bread, cubed

1 medium can (#2 size) crushed pineapple, undrained

Directions:

1. Cream butter and sugar together. Add eggs and beat well. Add crushed pineapple with juice. Fold in bread cubes.
2. Bake uncovered in greased casserole in a 350° F oven for 45 minutes to 1 hour until golden brown.

Esther Gallagher's Pistachio Coffee Cake

This coffee cake was a big hit during the 70's and 80's.

OOPS! I guess I'm really dating myself!! I think it's time to reintroduce this tasty treat to the 21st century. You are guaranteed to get rave reviews whenever you serve this cake. It is a nice addition to a Sunday Brunch!

Ingredients:

- Cake:
    - 1 box yellow cake mix
    - 1 box instant pistachio pudding
    - 4 eggs
    - ½ cup vegetable oil
    - 1 cup sour cream

- Topping:
    - ½ cup chopped nuts
    - 4 Tablespoons sugar
    - 1 Tablespoon cinnamon

Directions:

1. Place first five ingredients in bowl and beat with electric mixer for four minutes.
2. When well mixed, pour half of batter in a greased and floured tube pan.
3. Sprinkle with half of the topping mixture.
4. Gently spoon and spread rest of batter into pan and finish with remaining topping mixture.
5. Bake in a 350° F oven for 55-60 minutes.

Poached Eggs

Ingredients:

    12 large eggs

    1 Tablespoon distilled white vinegar

Directions:

1. Pour cold water into a 10-inch sauté pan to a depth of about 2 inches. Bring to a simmer, then reduce the heat so that the surface of the water barely shimmers. Add the vinegar.

2. Break four of the eggs into individual saucers, then gently slide them out one at a time into water and, with a large spoon, lift the white over the yolk. Repeat the lifting once or twice to completely enclose each yolk. Poach until the whites are set and the yolks feel soft when touched gently, 3 to 4 minutes.

3. Remove the eggs with a slotted spoon and either serve immediately or place in a shallow pan or large bowl of cold water.

4. Repeat with the remaining eggs, adding more water as needed to keep the depth at 2 inches, and bringing the water to a simmer before adding the eggs.

5. Reheat the eggs by slipping them into simmering water for 30 seconds to 1 minute.

We enjoy serving them hot with crab cakes.

PA Dutch Potato Pancakes

Ingredients:

    4 lbs. potatoes, peeled

    2 large onions

    1 egg

    1½ cups flour

    2 teaspoons baking powder

    1 teaspoon lemon juice

    Ground nutmeg

    Oil or vegetable shortening

    1 Tablespoon salt

    Sour cream

Directions:

1. Peel and quarter potatoes and onions
2. Finely shred the potatoes using a food processor or grinder
3. Finely shred the onions
4. Squeeze out excess liquid from shredded potatoes and onions
5. Mix shredded potatoes and onions with other ingredients. Form into pancakes
6. In a large skillet with oil/shortening fry pancakes until golden brown
7. Drain pancakes on paper towel and keep warm

    Serve with sour cream for topping

Brenda's St. Patrick's Day Scones

Ingredients:

Scones:

    4 cups flour

    1½ cups raisins

    1 cup sugar

    2 sticks butter, cut into small slices

    ½ teaspoon salt

    2 eggs

    4 teaspoons baking powder

    1 cup milk

Egg wash:

    1 egg

    1 Tablespoon milk

Directions:

1. Preheat oven to 350° F.
2. Whisk all dry ingredients together.
3. Gradually mix in raisins, distributing evenly.
4. Add butter in small cubes and mix in with fingers or pastry blender.
5. Whisk egg and milk together in a small bowl and gradually stir into flour mixture until dough forms.
6. Work dough with hands, but don't overwork.
7. Drop scant ½ cup amounts of dough onto 2 ungreased cookie sheets.
8. Make egg wash by beating egg and milk together.
9. Lightly brush each scone with egg wash.
10. Bake at 350° F for 20 - 25 minutes until lightly golden.

    Serve warm with butter and jam.

Pennsylvania Fried Scrapple

Serves approximately 8 hungry PA Dutchmen

Ingredients:

2 lbs original PA Scrapple, "imported" from PA
Butter or oil
Catsup or syrup

Directions:

Use your largest skillet on medium high heat and coat with butter or oil
Cut scrapple into ¼ to ½ inch slices
Fry until both sides are a golden brown
Serve with catsup or syrup

Swiss Cheese Scramble

I usually prepare this dish the day before and refrigerate overnight. If you choose to do this you will need to increase the cooking time to 25 - 30 minutes or until cheese is bubbly.

Also don't sprinkle with bacon until the last 5 - 10 minutes. This will prevent the bacon from becoming too brown.

This dish has always been a big hit whenever we serve it to our guests. Every summer for 29 years Ed's Mercyhurst students would come for brunch. A "real live teacher" was invited to share his/her experiences about teaching.

Ingredients:

- 12 - 14 slices bacon, fried crisp and crumbled
- 3 cups soft bread cubes (about 7 slices), with crusts removed
- 2½ cups milk
- 12 eggs, slightly beaten
- 1 teaspoon salt
- ¼ teaspoon pepper
- 3 Tablespoons butter
- ¾ lb. Swiss cheese, sliced
- 3 Tablespoons butter, melted
- ¾ cup bread crumbs

Directions:

1. Combine bread cubes and milk. Drain after 5 minutes. Combine drained milk with eggs, salt and pepper
2. Melt 3 Tablespoons butter in skillet. Add egg mixture and scramble until soft, but not quite fully cooked
3. Add soaked bread cubes and place in 13 x 9-inch baking dish
4. Arrange Swiss cheese slices on top of egg mixture
5. Combine melted butter and bread crumbs and sprinkle over cheese
6. Sprinkle bacon on top.
7. Bake in a 400° F oven for 15 - 18 minutes or until cheese bubbles. Serve immediately.

Grammie Jane's Waffles With Pecan and Banana Syrup

My grandkids demand this every time they come. They like to top the waffles with maple syrup, berries, and whipped cream.

Yield: 4 to 8 servings

Ingredients:

¼ pound (1 stick) plus 2 Tablespoons unsalted butter, melted

1 cup pecan pieces

2 medium-size ripe bananas, peeled and cut crosswise into ½-inch-thick slices

2 cups pure maple syrup

1½ cups all-purpose flour

⅓ cup ground pecans

⅓ cup sugar

1 Tablespoon baking powder

¼ teaspoon salt

2 large egg yolks

1 teaspoon pure vanilla extract

1¾ cups milk

2 large egg whites

Directions:

1. Heat 2 Tablespoons of the butter in a medium-size sauté pan over medium heat. Add the pecan pieces and cook, stirring, until golden, 2 to 3 minutes. Add the banana slices and syrup and bring to a simmer. Set aside and keep warm.

2. Combine the flour, sugar, baking powder, and salt in a medium-size mixing bowl.

3. In a separate bowl, beat the egg yolks and vanilla together. Add the milk and the 1 stick of melted butter to the egg mixture and whisk to combine.

4. Fold the flour mixture into the egg mixture. Stir until combined yet still slightly lumpy.

5. In a small mixing bowl whip the egg whites until stiff peaks form. Gently fold into the batter, leaving little fluffs.

6. If using a Belgian waffle iron, pour 1 cup of the batter onto the grids of a preheated and lightly greased waffle iron. (Regular waffle irons will take only about ½ cup.)

7. Close the lid. Do not open during cooking time. For the Belgian waffle iron, cook until golden and crisp, 3 to 4 minutes. Smaller waffle irons will take 1½ to 3 minutes.

Serve hot with the pecan and banana syrup.

Chef Note:

- You can make ahead except for the whipping of the egg whites.

Salads and Dressings

Asparagus Tomato Salad with Crabmeat

Makes 6 servings

Ingredients:

Salad:

- 1 pound fresh asparagus, washed and trimmed
- Salt
- Black pepper
- 2 Tablespoons olive oil
- 1 pound lump crab meat
- ¼ cup small diced red onions
- 1 medium Vadalia onion, shaved very thin
- 12 slices tomatoes, such as beefsteak or vine ripened (about ¼ in. thick)

Dressing:

- ½ cup extra virgin olive oil
- 2 Tablespoons minced shallots
- 1 teaspoon minced garlic
- Juice of 2 lemons
- ¼ cup finely chopped fresh herbs (such as basil, chervil, parsley, and tarragon)

Directions:

1. Preheat oven to 400° F.
2. Add asparagus to a pot of salted boiling water, cook for 2 minutes.
3. Remove asparagus from the water and place in a bowl of ice water (called "shocking") for 4 minutes, remove, and pat dry.
4. Toss asparagus with 2 Tablespoons of olive oil, season with salt and pepper, place on a baking sheet lined with parchment paper, and roast for 6 minutes.
5. Remove asparagus from oven and cool.
6. In a small mixing bowl whisk ½ cup extra virgin olive oil and lemon juice, to emulsify the vinaigrette (should turn cloudy). Add shallots and garlic. Season with salt and pepper. Whisk in herbs and set aside.
7. Toss the crab meat with ½ cup of the dressing, adding the red onions, again season with salt and pepper.
8. Season both sides of the tomatoes with salt and pepper.
9. Assemble: Arrange tomato slices on a plate, place asparagus over tomatoes, arrange the Vadalia onions over the asparagus, drizzle the remainder of the dressing, and finally mound the crab meat salad in the center.

Brenda's Dressing For Macaroni or Potato Salad

Simply use the ingredients from your favorite macaroni or potato salad or use Brenda's dressing instead. It's a crowd pleaser!

Ingredients:

- 1½ cups Miracle Whip™
- ½ cup sugar
- 2 Tablespoons yellow mustard
- 2 Tablespoons vinegar
- Salt & Pepper to taste

Directions:

1. Combine all ingredients and mix well

Doris Yost's Caesar Dressing

Ingredients:

- 1 pint mayonnaise
- 3 eggs
- ¾ teaspoon curry powder
- ¼ teaspoon garlic powder
- ½ cup parmesan cheese
- ½ teaspoon anchovy paste
- ½ package Lipton Onion Soup Mix™

Directions:

1. Combine above ingredients and mix well
Enjoy!

Note:

- Good to refrigerate in a sealed container for a month

Cole Slaw

Ingredients:

1 medium cabbage (about 2 pounds), outer leaves removed

> (You can use green cabbage, red cabbage, savoy cabbage, or Napa cabbage. For multi-colored or multi-textured coleslaw, use a combination of two varieties.)

3 medium carrots, peeled and shredded

¼ cup milk

¼ cup buttermilk

2½ Tablespoons lemon juice

1½ Tablespoons white or cider vinegar

2 Tablespoons Dijon or coarse-ground mustard

½ teaspoon salt

⅛ teaspoon pepper

Directions:

1. Quarter the cabbage through the core, and then cut out the core. Cut each quarter crosswise in half and finely shred
2. Place the shredded cabbage and shredded carrots in a very large bowl and toss to mix (you will have 6 to 8 cups)
3. In a separate bowl, stir the milk, buttermilk, lemon juice, vinegar, mustard, salt, and pepper together. Taste for acidity and seasoning and adjust for desired taste
4. Pour two-thirds of the dressing over the cabbage and carrot mixture, then mix well. If the coleslaw seems dry, add a little more of the dressing
5. Let sit in the refrigerator for about an hour to let the flavors mingle and the cabbage soften.

Deb's Dijon Vinaigrette Salad Dressing

Ingredients:

- ¾ cup salad oil
- ¼ cup Regina™ red wine vinegar
- ½ teaspoon garlic salt
- ¼ teaspoon black pepper
- 2 Tablespoons Grey Poupon™ Mustard

Directions:

1. Use the famous DGall whisk technique and delight all the tastebuds of your guests

Hollandaise Sauce

Makes one cup

Ingredients:

    4 egg yolks

    2 teaspoons fresh lemon juice

    1/8 teaspoon cayenne, or to taste

    2 sticks unsalted butter, melted

    1/2 teaspoon salt

Directions:

1. Whisk the egg yolks, lemon juice, and cayenne in the top of a double boiler, or in a stainless steel bowl set over a pot of simmering water (being careful not to let the bowl touch the water).

2. As soon as the egg yolks have thickened, remove the pot from the water and slowly add the melted butter a bit at a time, whisking continuously. Add the salt and adjust the seasoning to taste.

   Serve immediately or keep warm, covered, over a pot of simmering water, for a short time.

Brenda's Hot Bacon Dressing

Ingredients:

    Salad mixture:

        1 head lettuce

        Other salad garnishing, such as onion, graded cheese, hard boiled egg, chick peas

    Dressing:

        1 egg

        10 strips bacon

        ½ cup cider vinegar

        ½ cup sugar

Directions:

1. Prepare base salad mixture and refrigerate
2. Fry bacon and cut or crumble — save bacon grease
3. Beat egg and add vinegar and sugar, then pour into hot frying pan with bacon grease
4. Stir until thick and add a bit of water if too thick
5. Add crumbled bacon to dressing and serve with salad mixture

Brenda's Layered Salad

Ingredients:

    1 head lettuce

    2 cups shredded carrots

    1 red onion, sliced thinly

    ½ cup diced celery

    ½ cup diced sweet peppers

    1 can thinly sliced water chestnuts, drained

    20 oz. frozen peas — do not thaw

    ¼ cup grated Parmesan cheese

    2 cups mayonnaise

    1 Tablespoon granulated sugar

    1 cup grated cheddar cheese

    ½ lb. bacon, cooked and crumbled (could substitute ½ cup bacon bits)

Directions:
1. Break lettuce into small pieces and place into a deep bowl or pan.
2. Spread layers of ingredients on top as follows:
   - Diced celery
   - Diced sweet pepper
   - Thinly sliced onion
   - Frozen peas
   - Grated Parmesan cheese
3. Spread with mayonnaise like frosting a cake
4. Sprinkle with sugar
5. Top with grated Cheddar cheese and crumbled bacon
6. **Do Not Stir!**
7. Cover tightly with Saran wrap and chill 8 hours or more before serving

Mango Salsa

Ingredients:

- 2 large ripe mangoes
- 1 small cucumber
- 2 scallions or spring onions
- 1 medium jalapeno pepper
- 2 medium limes
- ½ teaspoon salt
- Pinch of cayenne pepper

Optional Ingredients:

- 1 medium bell pepper
- ¼ fresh cilantro or parsley or mint

Directions:

1. Rinse veggies and fruit Peel mangoes and cut mango flesh from the pits
2. Cut cucumber in half lengthwise and remove seeds. If using bell pepper, cut in half lengthwise, then remove stems and seeds
3. Dice mangoes, cucumber, and bell pepper. Finely chop scallions
4. Rinse and chop cilantro, if using
5. Cut limes in half. Squeeze juice from lime and discard seeds
6. Add all ingredients into bowl with lime juice and mix well
7. Cover and refrigerate for at least one hour before serving.

Chef Note:

- If you don't want to use mangos or you want more fruit in your salsa, add pineapple, peaches, tomatoes etc.

Carolina Shrimp Salad with Avocado

Ingredients:

- 2 avocados, halved, pitted, and peeled
- 2 cups shrimp, boiled
- 9-oz. can crushed pineapple
- ⅔ cup sour cream
- 1 cup celery diced
- 1 head lettuce, shredded
- 4 oz. shredded Swiss cheese
- 1 teaspoon salt

Directions:

1. Mix together the shrimp, celery, crushed pineapple, sour cream, and salt.
2. Chill until firm.
3. Arrange avocado halves on a bed of the shredded lettuce
4. Spoon mixture onto the avocados
5. Sprinkle cheese on top.
6. Keep cold until ready to serve.

Tomato Salad

Yield: 3 cups

Ingredients:

    1 cup roasted sweet corn

    ½ pint red tear drop tomatoes, stemmed, washed and sliced in half

    ½ pint yellow tear drop tomatoes, stemmed, washed and sliced in half

    ½ cup red onions, minced

    2 Tablespoons fresh parsley leaves, chopped

    1 Tablespoon freshly-squeezed lime juice

    1 Tablespoon freshly-squeezed lemon juice

    Salt

    Freshly ground black pepper

Directions:

1. Combine the corn, tomatoes, onions, parsley, lime juice and lemon juice. Mix well
2. Season with salt and pepper

    Serve cold or at room temperature

Crockpot Soups

Lisa's Broccoli Cheese Soup

Ingredients:

- 2 16-ounce packages frozen chopped broccoli
- 2 10¾-ounce cans condensed cheddar cheese soup
- 2 12-ounce cans evaporated milk
- ½ teaspoon salt
- ¼ teaspoon pepper

Directions:

1. Combine all ingredients in greased 4 or 6-quart slow cooker.
2. Cover and cook on high heat 2 - 3 hours or on low heat 4 - 5 hours

Lisa's Chicken and Wild Rice Soup

Ingredients:
- 1 can cream of chicken soup
- 2 cups cooked chicken, chopped
- 1 cup carrots, shredded
- 1 cup celery, diced
- 2 packages long grain and wild rice mix, with seasoning packets
- 5 cups chicken broth
- 5 cups water

Directions:
1. Combine all ingredients in a greased 4½ to 6-quart slow cooker.
2. Cover and cook on low heat 4 - 6 hours or until rice is done.
3. About half way through, stir the soup to make sure the rice cooks evenly.
4. Do not overcook.

Lisa's Creamy Corn and Potato Chowder

Makes about 5 quarts

Ingredients:

- 6 16-oz. cans creamed corn
- ½ cup chopped onion
- 12-oz. can evaporated milk
- 2 cups chicken broth
- 7-oz. box dry mash potato mix flavored with sour cream and chives
- 2 cups water

Directions:

1. Combine all ingredients in crock pot and stir well
2. Cover and cook on low for 6 hours or high for 3 hours

Note:
- I substitute homemade mashed potatoes and chives for the last 3 ingredients (chicken broth, dry mash potatoes mix, and water)

Lisa's Crockpot Mexican Green Chile Pork Stew

Ingredients:

- 1½ pounds boneless pork shoulder, cut into 1-inch cubes
- 2 medium baking potatoes or sweet potatoes, peeled and cut into large chunks
- 1 cup chopped onion
- 4-ounce can diced green chiles
- 1 cup frozen corn
- 2 teaspoons sugar
- 2 teaspoons cumin or chile powder
- 1 teaspoon dried oregano
- 10-ounce jar *salsa verde* (green salsa)

Directions:

1. Place pork, potatoes, onion, chiles and corn into 4½ quart crockpot
2. Stir sugar, cumin and oregano into salsa and poor over pork and vegetables. Stir gently to mix.
3. Cover cook on low 6 to 8 hours or on high 4 to 5 hours, or until pork is tender

   Serve stew over hot rice and garnish with cilantro

Westley Football Tailgate Chili

Makes a mild chili. Have hot sauces available to add for those who prefer a hot chili taste.

Makes 12 servings

Ingredients:

- 2 40-oz. cans kidney beans
- 2 24-oz. jars / cans spaghetti sauce (your favorite brand)
- 1 pound bulk sausage
- 2 pounds lean ground beef
- 1 pound shredded cheddar or other favorite cheese
- 1 large or 2 small sweet onions, diced
- 1 each sweet red and yellow bell peppers, diced (can substitute green peppers)
- 4 oz. fresh mushrooms, sliced
- 3 cloves garlic, minced
- 3 Tablespoons brown sugar

Directions:

1. Clean and dice onion, peppers, and mushrooms
2. Use a separate frying pan to cook the sausage and ground beef; break up meats into small chunks and drain fat before adding to the chili pot.
3. While the meat is browning, drain the kidney beans and rinse with water
4. Add kidney beans, cooked meats, and spaghetti sauce to a large crock-pot or slow simmer in a large pot on the stove. Slow cook to avoid boiling chili mixture
5. Add onion, peppers, mushrooms, garlic, and brown sugar to chili pot and stir ingredients together
6. Cook chili mixture until onion and peppers have softened, approximately 90 minutes

Have shredded cheddar cheese to top off a served bowl of chili

Proszkow Vegetarian Chili

Ingredients:

3 packages Morningstar Recipe Burger Crumbles™

1 chopped medium yellow onion

1 cup chili powder

2 to 4 chili peppers (optional)

15.5-oz. can light red kidney beans

15.5-oz. can black beans

6-oz. can tomato paste

3 15.5-oz cans tomato sauce

14.5-oz. can diced tomatoes

crushed red pepper to taste

salt and pepper to taste

3 to 6 Tablespoons butter

Directions:

1. Mix beans, tomato paste, tomato sauce, diced tomatoes, chili powder, red pepper flakes, salt, and pepper together in a crock pot. Do not turn on yet

2. Melt 1 to 2 Tablespoons butter in medium frying pan, then add half the onion and fry for about 2 to 3 minutes. Add 1 bag of frozen burger crumbles and sauté until softened. Add to crock pot

3. Repeat the previous step using butter. remaining onion, and second bag of burger crumbles, then add to crockpot

4. For third bag of burger crumbles, melt 1 to 2 Tablespoons of butter in frying pan, then add burger crumbles and sauté until softened. Add to crock pot

5. Mix all together and cover. Cooking on high for 6 hours, stirring intermittently

6. Wait at least 4 hours for everything to blend together

Lisa's Santa Fe Cheese Soup

Makes 6-8 servings

Ingredients:

    1 pound Velveeta™, cubed

    1 pound ground beef, browned and drained.

    1 can whole kernel corn, with liquid

    1 can kidney beans, with liquid

    1 can diced tomatoes with green chilies, with liquid

    1 can stewed tomatoes, diced, with liquid

    1 envelope taco seasoning mix

Directions:
1. Combine all ingredients in greased 4½ to 6-quart slow cooker
2. Cover and cook on high heat 3 hours or on low heat 4 - 5 hours
   Serve with corn chips

Lisa's Crockpot Tomato and Rice Soup with Pesto

Ingredients:
- 1 cup chopped onion
- 1 cup shredded carrot
- 3 stalks celery with leaves, chopped
- 1 can Italian-style stewed tomatoes
- 6-ounce can Italian-style tomato paste
- ½ teaspoon dried oregano, crushed
- ¼ teaspoon dried thyme, crushed
- ¼ teaspoon pepper
- 2 cups water
- 2 cups chicken broth or vegetable broth
- 1 cup quick-cooking rice
- ¼ cup pesto
- Grated Parmesan cheese

Directions:
1. In 3 to 4-quart slow cooker combine onion, carrot, celery, undrained tomatoes, tomato paste, oregano, thyme, and pepper
2. Stir in water and chicken or vegetable broth
3. Cover and cook on low heat setting for 8 to 10 hours or high heat setting for 4 to 5 hours
4. Stir in rice
5. Cover and let stand 6 to 7 minutes or until rice is tender
6. Stir in pesto

Ladle soup into bowls. Sprinkle with grated Parmesan cheese if desired.

Lisa's Turkey and Rice Soup

Ingredients:

    1 small onion, chopped

    1 cup celery, diced

    1 to 3 cups cooked turkey, diced

    1 cup converted white rice, uncooked

    4 cups water

    1 jar turkey gravy

    ½ teaspoon salt

    ½ teaspoon pepper

Directions:

1. Combine all ingredients in greased 3½ to 5-quart slow cooker
2. Cover and cook on low heat 5 to 7 hours or until rice is done. Do not overcook

Note:
- I use leftover rice and cut the cooking time down to 4 hours. I have never been able to cook rice in slow cooker and have it come out nicely.

Westley Ham and Bean Soup

Ingredients:

    Leftover ham butt, preferably from a honey-baked ham (can substitute 2 ham shanks)

    1 large sweet onion, diced

    1 pound thinly sliced baby carrots

    96 oz. prepared navy or northern beans, including liquid

        (I prefer 2 jars of Randall™ fully-cooked and ready-to-eat beans. If you are using dried beans, follow directions to hydrate the beans.)

    2 Tablespoons brown sugar (may need to double if ham butt is unsweetened)

    Salt and pepper to taste

Directions:

1. Slice and dice carrots and onion.
2. Layer bottom of your crock pot with some of the sliced carrots, onions, and beans
3. Add ham butt and cover ham with the remainder of the sliced carrots and onions. Top off with enough beans and residual bean jar liquid to leave 2 inches space below the rim of the crock pot to facilitate removing the ham butt later
4. Set crock pot on high and slow cook for about 2½ hours
5. Pull ham butt out to cool
6. Add remainder of beans to crock pot, lower heat to medium
7. Let ham butt cool, then cut the ham into bite sized soup pieces. Add cut ham to soup

Season to taste

Note:

- If you are cooking in a pot on top of the stove, adjust the burner heat to low or slow cooking temperatures for your stove and cook for about 2½ hours. Do not boil the soup.

Soups and Stews

Lisa's Chicken Vegetable Rice Soup

Ingredients:

½ pound skinless chicken breasts   cubed into bite size pieces

1½ cups chicken broth

1½ cups water

2 cups assorted cut-up fresh vegetables, such as sliced carrots, broccoli flowerets and chopped red peppers or 1 package frozen mixed vegetables, thawed

1 envelope Good Seasons™ Italian salad dressing mix

1 cup minute white rice, uncooked

Directions:

1. Cook and stir skinless chicken breasts in large saucepan sprayed with no stick cooking spray until cooked through, about 8 minutes
2. Stir in broth, water, vegetables, and salad dressing mix.
3. Bring to a boil. Reduce heat to low and cover. Simmer 7 to 9 minutes or until vegetables are tender (if using frozen vegetables, simmer 6 minutes)
4. Stir in rice. Cover. Remove from heat. Let stand 5 minutes

Dutch Chicken Corn Noodle Soup

Ingredients:

    1 large stewing chicken

    1 large sweet onion, coarsely chopped

    5 stalks celery, split and coarsely chopped

    16-oz. bag PA Dutch butter noodles

    2 cans whole kernel corn, drained

    1 large container chicken broth

    Salt and pepper to taste

    1 hard-boiled egg per serving, sliced

    Fresh parsley for garnish

Directions:

1. Remove giblets and rinse chicken under cold running water
2. Place chicken and giblets in large stockpot and cover with 2 inches of water
3. Add chopped onions and celery, bring stock pot to a boil
4. Skim off and discard any foam rising to the surface
5. Lower heat to a simmer and cook for about 2 hours
6. Remove chicken and giblets and let cool
7. Add noodles and whole kernel corn to the stock and simmer, stirring occasionally
8. Pick the chicken meat off the bones, cut up into bite-sized pieces, and return to stock.
9. Add more chicken broth to supplement stock, as noodles will soak up a lot of broth.
10. Season with salt & pepper to taste

    Serve with sliced hard boiled egg and parsley garnish

Edward J. Gallagher's Chicken Corn Soup

This is a traditional Pennsylvania Dutch recipe. I always make several batches when fresh corn is plentiful. "Mmmmm. Mmmmm, GOOD!!"

Ingredients:

- 4 lb. stewing chicken
- About 5 quarts water
- 1 large onion, cut in half
- 3 medium carrots, peeled
- 2 to 3 stalks celery with leaves
- 10 sprigs fresh parsley
- 12 black peppercorns
- Salt to taste
- 12 ears of corn, husked, cleaned, and cut off of the cobs
- 6 eggs, hard boiled and diced

Directions:

1. Rinse the chicken under cold running water. Place chicken, carrots, celery, parsley, peppercorns and salt in an 8 to 10 quart stockpot. Pour in the cold water and bring to a boil over high heat. Boil for a few minutes and you will see foam rising to the surface. Skim off and discard the foam, lower the heat to a strong simmer, and cook for at least 2½ hours, occasionally skimming the foam and fat from the surface.

2. Strain the broth through a very fine sieve or a colander. Season the broth lightly with salt, as needed. Set the chicken and carrots aside to cool. Discard the celery, parsley, and peppercorns. Return the chicken broth to the pot. Once chicken and carrots have cooled, cut up chicken into bite-size pieces and slice the carrots. Set aside.

3. Add corn kernels to chicken broth; bring to a boil and cook for about 10 minutes or until corn is tender. Next, stir in cut up chicken, carrots, and diced eggs. Heat soup until hot. Adjust seasonings and serve!

Clam Chowder

Ingredients:

    4 dozen cherrystone clams, scrubbed

    About 2 cups low-sodium chicken broth

    6 ounces sliced bacon, cut crosswise into ½-inch pieces

    2 medium sweet onions, cut into ¼-inch dice

    3 carrots, cut into ¼-inch dice

    2 celery ribs, cut into ¼-inch dice

    Kosher salt

    ⅛ teaspoon cayenne pepper

    1 bay leaf

    ½ cup all-purpose flour

    3 medium red potatoes (1¼ pounds), peeled and cut into ½-inch dice

    2 ears of corn, kernels cut from the cobs

    1 teaspoon Old Bay™ seasoning

    1 cup half-and-half

    ½ cup finely chopped flat-leaf parsley

    1 teaspoon Worcestershire sauce

    ¼ teaspoon Tabasco sauce

    Freshly ground pepper

Directions:

1. In a large soup pot, add clams and 4 cups water. Bring to a simmer over moderately high heat, cover, and cook until the clams start to open, about 4 minutes. As the clams open, transfer them to a large bowl to cool; discard any clams that do not open.

2. Strain the clam liquid into a large measuring cup (there should be 5½ cups of liquid). Add enough chicken broth to make 7½ cups.

3. Wipe out the soup pot and place over moderate heat. Add the bacon and cook, stirring occasionally, until crisp, about 12 minutes. Set bacon aside

4. Add the onions, carrots, celery, 2 teaspoons salt, cayenne, and bay leaf. Cook until the vegetables are soft, about 10 minutes.

5. Stir in the flour and cook until it begins to stick to the bottom of the pan, about 2 minutes.

6. Stir in the clam-broth mixture and bring to a boil. Add potatoes, corn, and Old Bay™ and simmer over moderately low heat until potatoes are tender, about 15 minutes.

7. Remove the clams from their shells and coarsely chop them.

8. Stir in the half-and-half, parsley, Worcestershire sauce, and Tabasco.

9. Remove chowder broth from the heat and stir in the clams. Discard the bay leaf and season the chowder with salt and pepper.

Ladle the chowder into bowls and serve.

Westley Corn Chowder

Ingredients:

    6 slices raw bacon, diced

    ½ large sweet onion, diced

    1½ cups peeled diced potato in ½-inch cubes

    ½ red bell pepper, diced

    1 teaspoon thyme

    Black pepper to taste

    2 cups chicken broth

    3 cups corn (fresh or frozen)

    1½ cups diced ham

    2 Tablespoons flour

    1½ cups milk

Directions:

1. Add bacon and onion to a pot over medium high heat. Cook until onion is translucent. Remove bacon and excess bacon fat
2. Add potato, red pepper, thyme, pepper and chicken broth. Bring to a boil, reduce heat and let simmer 8 minutes
3. Add corn and ham. Simmer an additional 7 minutes or until potatoes are cooked through
4. Stir together milk and flour. Add into the pot mixture and bring to a boil while stirring. Let boil 2 minutes

Garnish servings with crumbled bacon and chopped chives or scallions

Notes:
- Recommend using fresh corn in season. Cut kernels off cobs and scrape the corn cobs with the back of a knife to collect the corn milk.

Lobster and Corn Chowder

Makes about 10 cups
Serves 10 as a first course or five or six as a main course

Ingredients:

- 3 live hard-shell lobsters (1¼ pounds each)
- 3 medium ears yellow or bi-color corn
- 4 ounces slab (unsliced) bacon, rind removed and cut into ⅓-inch dice
- 4 Tablespoons unsalted butter
- 1 large onion (10 ounces) cut into ¾-inch dice
- 2 to 3 sprigs fresh thyme, leaves removed and chopped (1 teaspoon)
- 2 teaspoons Hungarian paprika
- 1½ pounds Yukon Gold or other all-purpose potatoes, peeled and cut into ½-inch dice cubes
- 1½ cups heavy cream (or up to 2 cups, if desired)

Kosher or sea salt and freshly ground black pepper ed

For garnish:

- 2 Tablespoons chopped fresh Italian parsley
- 2 Tablespoons minced fresh chives

Directions:

1. Fill an 8 to 10-quart stockpot two-thirds full with salted tap water. Bring to a rolling boil. Carefully drop Lobsters one at a time into the boiling water. Cook for exactly four minutes from the time the last lobster went in. Using a pair of long tongs, remove the lobsters from the pot and let them cool to room temperature

2. Pick all the meat from the tails, knuckles and claws. Remove the intestinal tract from the tail and the cartilage from the claws. Dice the meat into ¾-inch cubes. Cover and refrigerate until ready to use. Using the carcasses (bodies), and leftover shells, make a lobster stock (Recipe is below). The stock will take about 1½ hours to cook. Strain the stock; you should have 4 cups

3. Meanwhile, husk the corn. Carefully remove most of the silk by hand and then rub each ear with a dry towel to finish the job. Cut the kernels from the cobs and reserve. You should get about 2 cups. Break the cobs in half and add them to the simmering stock

4. Heat a 4 to 6-quart heavy pot over low heat and add the bacon. Once it has rendered a few Tablespoons of fat, increase the heat to medium and cook until the bacon is crisp golden brown. Pour off all but 1 Tablespoon of the fat, leaving the bacon in the pot

5. Add the butter, onion and thyme and sauté, stirring occasionally with a wooden spoon, for about 8 minutes, until the onion is softened but not browned. Add the paprika and cook 1 minute longer, stirring frequently.

continued on following page

continued from previous page

6. Add the potatoes, corn kernels, and the reserved lobster stock. The stock should just barley cover the potatoes; if it doesn't, add enough water to cover. Turn up the heat and bring to a boil. Cover the pot and cook the potatoes vigorously for about 12 minutes, until they are soft on the outside but still firm in the center. If the broth hasn't thickened lightly, smash a few potatoes against the side of the pot and cook a minute or two longer to release their starch

7. Remove the pot from the heat; stir in the lobster meat and cream, and season to taste with salt and pepper. If you are not serving the chowder within the hour, let it cool a bit, then refrigerate; cover the chowder after it is chilled completely. Otherwise, let it sit at room temperature for up to an hour, allowing the flavors to meld

8. When ready to serve, reheat the chowder over low heat; don't let it boil. Use a slotted spoon to mound the lobster, onions, potatoes, and corn in the center of large soup plates or shallow bowls, making sure they are evenly divided, and ladle the creamy broth around. Sprinkle with the chopped parsley and minced chives

Ingredients for Lobster Stock:

    2 pounds lobster carcasses and shells

    2 quarts water

    1 cup dry white wine

    1 cup chopped tomatoes with their juice (fresh or canned)

    2 medium onions, thinly sliced

    2 stalks celery, thinly sliced

    2 small carrots, thinly sliced

    4 cloves garlic, crushed

    4 sprigs fresh thyme

    2 dried bay leaves

    ¼ teaspoon fennel seeds

    1 teaspoon black peppercorns

    Kosher or sea salt

Directions for Lobster Stock:

1. Split the lobster carcasses lengthwise and remove the head sac from each one. Place the carcasses, shells and tomalley (lobster's liver) in a 6 to 8-quart stockpot, cover with the water, and bring to a boil, skim the white scum from the surface of the stock. Reduce the heat so the stock is cooking at a fast, steady simmer

2. Add the wine, tomatoes, onions, celery, carrots, garlic, thyme, bay leaves, fennel seeds and peppercorns, and let the stock simmer and cook down for about 1 hour. Add a little water if the stock falls below the lobster shells

3. Season the stock lightly with salt. Taste for a rich flavor. If it seems light, simmer for about 20 minutes longer. Strain the stock with a fine-mesh strainer. If you are not going to be using it within the hour, chill it as quickly as possible. Cover the broth after it has completely cooled and keep refrigerated for up to three days, or freeze for up to two months. Makes about 1 quart

Ed's French Onion Soup (Soupe à l'Oignon)

Serves 6 to 8

Ingredients:

Soup:

- 4 Tablespoons butter
- 2 Tablespoons vegetable oil
- 2 lbs. onons, thinly sliced (about 7 cups)
- 1 teaspoon salt
- 3 Tablespoons flour
- 2 quarts beef stock, fresh or canned, or beef and chicken stock combined

Croûtes

- 12 to 16 one-inch slices French bread
- 2 teaspoons olive oil
- 1 garlic clove, cut
- 1 cup grated swiss cheese or a combination of swiss and parmesan

Directions:

1. In a heavy 4 to 5 qt. saucepan or a soup kettle, melt the butter with the oil over moderate heat. Stir in the onions and 1 teaspoon salt, and cook uncovered over low heat, stirring occasionally, for 20 to 30 minutes, or until the onions are a rich golden brown. Sprinkle flour over the onions and cook, stirring, for 2 or 3 minutes. Remove the pan from the heat. In a separate saucepan, bring the stock to a simmer, then stir the hot stock into the onions. Return the soup to low heat and simmer, partially covered, for another 30 or 40 minutes, occasionally skimming off the fat. Taste for seasoning, and add salt and pepper if needed.

2. While the soup simmers, make the croûtes. Preheat the oven to 325° F. Spread the slices of bread in one layer on a baking sheet and bake for 15 minutes. With a pastry brush, lightly coat both sides of each slice with olive oil,. Then turn the slices over and bake for another 15 minutes or until the bread is completely dry and lightly browned. Rub each slice with the cut garlic clove and set aside.

To serve, place the croûtes in a large tureen or individual soup bowls and ladle the soup over them. Pass the grated cheese separately.

ALTERNATIVE:

- To make onion soup gratineé, preheat the oven to 375° F. Ladle the soup into an oven-proof tureen or individual soup bowls, top with croûtes, and spread the grated cheese on top. Bake for 10 to 20 minutes, or until the cheese has melted, then slide the soup under a hot broiler for a minute or two to brown the top.

Recipe courtesy of *The Cooking of Provincial France,* ©Time Life Cookbooks

Potato and Leek Soup

Ingredients:
- 2 Tablespoons vegetable oil
- 3 large leeks, white and pale green parts only, wash well
- 1 medium onion, diced
- 1 large clove garlic, minced
- 4 carrots, diced
- 4 cups chicken stock
- 2 teaspoons pepper
- 1 bay leaf
- 2 pounds potatoes, peeled and diced
- 2½ cups heavy whipping cream
- 3 Tablespoons cornstarch mixed in ¼ cup cold water
- Salt to taste
- Crispy fried onions, optional
- ¼ cup fresh parsley

Directions:
1. In a large stock pot, heat oil over medium heat
2. Slice leeks into ⅛ inch slices
3. Add leeks, onion, garlic, and carrots. Sauté until tender, approx. 10 minutes
4. Add potatoes, chicken stock, and bay leaf. Simmer until potatoes are tender
5. Stir in heavy cream and let simmer for another 5 minutes
6. Add cornstarch mixture a little at a time until the soup has thickened sufficiently to coat the back of a spoon
7. Remove and discard the bay leaf

Serve in bowls topped with fried onions and sprinkling of parsley

Consider shredded cheese and chopped spring onions for garnishes

Seafood Gumbo

Yield: 6 to 8 servings

Ingredients:

¾ cup vegetable oil

¾ cup all-purpose flour

2 cups chopped onions

1 cup chopped bell peppers

1 cup chopped celery

2 teaspoons salt

1 teaspoon cayenne pepper

3 bay leaves

1 Tablespoon minced garlic

1 bottle amber or dark lager beer

8 cups shrimp stock, at room temperature

6 gumbo crabs, broken in half (optional)

1 pound medium shrimp, peeled and deveined

1 pound lump crabmeat, picked over for shells and cartilage

2 dozen oysters, shucked, with their liquor

½ pound cooked crawfish tails

¼ cup chopped green onions

¼ cup chopped parsley

3 cups white long-grain rice, cooked

Filé powder to taste

Directions:

1. Heat the oil in a large cast-iron Dutch oven or stock pot over medium heat. Add the flour and, stirring constantly with a large wooden spoon, cook to make a dark brown roux, the color of chocolate, about 30 to 40 minutes.
2. Add the onions, bell peppers, celery, salt, cayenne, and bay leaves. Cook, stirring, until soft, about 5 minutes. Add the garlic and cook, stirring, for 30 seconds. Add the beer, stir to blend, and cook for 1 minute. Add the stock and mix to blend with the roux.
3. Add the crabs and simmer, uncovered, stirring occasionally, for 1½ hours. Add the shrimp and crabmeat and cook for 10 minutes.
4. Add the oysters, crawfish, green onions, and parsley and cook until the edges of the oysters curl, 2 to 3 minutes. Remove from the heat and discard the bay leaves.

To serve, spoon rice into the center of the serving bowls and top with the gumbo. Serve with filé powder passed at the table for guests to thicken the gumbo to their personal taste.

Sharon's Creamy Winter Vegetable Soup

Ingredients:

Soup:

¼ cup extra-virgin olive oil

3 to 4 garlic cloves, chopped or grated

2 carrots, thinly sliced

2 ribs celery with leafy tops, cut into ¼-inch dice

2 leeks, halved and sliced into ¼-inch pieces

2 parsnips, thinly sliced

2 medium starchy potatoes, peeled and cut into ½-inch dice

1 bulb fennel, cut into ¼-inch dice

1 small butternut squash, peeled and cut into ½-inch dice

Salt and freshly ground black pepper

Bundle of fresh herbs such as parsley, sage, thyme, marjoram or rosemary

½ cup dry white wine

2 cups chicken or vegetable stock

4 Tablespoons butter

4 Tablespoons all-purpose flour

3 cups whole milk

Freshly grated nutmeg, to taste

2 large fresh bay leaves

Cheesy Croutons:

4 Tablespoons butter

2 Tablespoons extra-virgin olive oil

2 large cloves garlic, crushed

4 cups diced stale white peasant-style bread

continued on following page

continued from previous page

    1 cup grated Parmigiano-Reggiano cheese

Directions:

For the soup:

1. Heat the olive oil in a large soup pot or Dutch oven over medium-high heat. Add the garlic, carrots, celery, leeks, parsnips, potatoes, fennel, and squash as you chop them and sprinkle with some salt and pepper. Nestle the bay leaves and herb bundle into the vegetables, partially cover, and cook until softened, stirring occasionally, 10 minutes.

2. Pour in the wine and reduce until almost evaporated. Then add the stock, bring to a boil, and then turn down to a simmer.

3. Meanwhile, melt the butter in a medium saucepan over medium to medium-high heat, and then whisk in the flour 1 minute. Whisk in the milk and season with salt, pepper, and nutmeg. Cook until the sauce thickens enough to coat the back of a spoon.

4. Pour the thickened milk mixture into the simmering vegetable soup, stir to combine and simmer a couple of minutes.

For the Cheesy Croutons:

1. Preheat the oven to 350° F

2. Heat the butter and oil in a large skillet over medium to medium-high heat

3. Stir in the garlic 1 minute, and then add the bread and toast until golden, stirring occasionally

4. Transfer to baking sheet and dress with the cheese

5. Bake to set the cheese and further dry out the croutons, 10 to 12 minutes

Remove the herb bundle and bay leaves from the soup and serve with the croutons

Chef Notes:

- Cool and store the soup in the refrigerator or freezer for a make-ahead meal. Bring to room temperature before reheating over medium heat. Store the croutons in foil or a cookie tin until ready to use.

Brenda's Award-Wining Chicken Pot Pie

Ingredients:

- 1 large stewing chicken
- 1 large sweet onion, coarsely chopped
- 5 stalks celery, split and coarsely chopped
- 1 large container of chicken broth
- Salt and pepper to taste
- Fresh parsley for garnish

Directions:

1. Rinse chicken under cold running water
2. Place chicken in large stockpot and cover chicken with 2 inches of water
3. Add chopped onion and celery, and bring stock pot to a boil
4. Skim off and discard any foam rising to the surface
5. Lower heat to a simmer and cook for about 2 hours
6. While chicken is cooking, make the pot pie dough *(see recipe on next page)*
7. Remove the chicken from the stock pot and let chicken cool
8. Return stock pot to a boil
9. Gently add dough squares into boiling chicken broth, stirring occasionally
10. Cook about 30 minutes until dough squares are tender, continuing to stir occasionally
11. Reduce heat to simmer
12. Pick the chicken meat off the bones, cut into bite-sized pieces, and return to stock
13. Dough will soak up a lot of stock liquid. If necessary, add chicken broth to supplement the amount of stock
14. Cover pot and simmer for another 5 minutes until chicken is re-heated
15. Season with salt and pepper to taste

Serve with parsley garnish

Dough For Brenda's Award-Wining Chicken Pot Pie

Ingredients:

    4 eggs

    ¾ cup milk

    1 teaspoon salt

    6 cups flour

Directions:

1. Beat the eggs, then add the milk and salt
2. Gradually mix the flour into the egg mixture until well blended
3. Gather the dough into a ball and knead until it is tender, smooth, and elastic
4. Divide dough into workable amounts; then on a lightly floured work surface, roll out the dough into a ⅛-inch thick sheet
5. Cut sheet into 1½-inch squares

Cowboy Stew

Ingredients:

    2 cups potatoes, cut into ½-inch cubes

    6 slices bacon

    1 cup sweet onion, diced

    ½ cup green pepper, chopped

    ¼ clove fresh garlic, minced

    1 teaspoon salt

    ¼ teaspoon pepper

    1 teaspoon chili powder

    1 can whole kernel corn, drained

    1 can kidney beans, drained

    1½ lbs. ground beef

    2 cans diced tomatoes

Directions:
1. Boil cubed potatoes in salt water until soft, set aside
2. Cook bacon until crisp. Drain, crumble, and set aside
3. Sauté onion, peppers, and garlic in bacon drippings until tender
4. Add ground beef and cook until browned. Drain fat
5. Add tomatoes and spices. Cover and simmer for 30 minutes
6. Add cooked potatoes, corn, and kidney beans. Simmer for 15 minutes

Serve with a sprinkle of bacon

Barley Jambalaya

Ingredients:

- 1 cup instant pearl barley
- 4 cups water
- 2 bay leaves
- 3 medium onions
- 2 medium celery stalks
- 1 medium green, red, yellow, or orange bell pepper
- 2 medium cloves garlic
- 1 Tablespoon canola oil
- 4 ounces ground turkey
- 2 14½ oz. cans diced tomatoes, no salt added
- 1 teaspoon salt
- ½ teaspoon ground cayenne pepper
- 1½ Tablespoons dried oregano
- 1 teaspoon ground black pepper

Directions:

1. In advance: rinse barley under cold water in a colander. Then bring barley, water, and bay leaves to a boil in a medium pot over high heat. Reduce heat to low and cover. Cook barley until tender and water is absorbed, drain barley. Set aside
2. Peel, rinse and dice onions. Rinse and dice celery and pepper. Peel and mince garlic
3. In a large pot over medium high heat, heat oil. Add onions, celery, pepper and garlic to pot Mix well. Cook until veggies are soft. About 5 minutes
4. Add ground turkey. Cook until turkey is cooked through, about 5 minutes
5. Add tomatoes and their juices. Bring to a simmer.
6. Add spices. Stir to combine. Cover and reduce heat. Cook at a low simmer for 15 minutes.
7. Add previously-cooked barley to the mixture. Stir to combine. Add more water or broth if needed. Cook over low heat to blend flavors.
8. Remove bay leaf and serve

Chef's Notes:

- Use turkey sausage, or soy sausage instead of ground turkey or tofu.
- When doubling this recipe, do not double cayenne pepper unless you prefer a very spicy dish.

Westley Mild Jambalaya

Yield: approximately 12 servings

Ingredients:

- 2 pounds medium shrimp or chicken breast
- 2 pounds sweet Italian sausage
- 2 boxes Zatarain's™ jambalaya rice mixture
- 1 large sweet onion, chopped
- 1 sweet red or yellow pepper (half red and half yellow gives best result), chopped
- 3 cloves garlic, minced
- 16-oz can tomato sauce
- 4 cups chicken broth

Directions:

1. Steam or boil shrimp; shell and de-vein shrimp; cut shrimp in half and set aside (or saute chicken and cut into bite-size pieces)
2. Cut Italian sausage into chunks; fry sausage chunks in a large (5 quart) pot, and remove from pot
3. Sauté onion, pepper, and garlic in sausage fat until slightly translucent
4. Add jambalaya rice mix including seasoning mix packet, chicken broth, and tomato sauce.
5. Bring mixture to a boil while stirring, then reduce to low heat.
6. Add cooked sausage and shrimp/chicken; stir, cover, and simmer for 25 minutes.
7. Remove from heat and let stand covered for 5 minutes

Fluff jambalaya and serve

Have hot sauce available for guests who want to "heat up" their jambalaya

Ed's Sausage Stew

This is good with Bisquick™ dumplings

Ingredients:

    Sausage, cut into 1-inch pieces

    Cooking oil

    Beef or chicken broth

    Potatoes, cubed

    Frozen peas

    Salt and pepper to taste

Directions:

    Brown sausage in a little oil in a large stock pot

    Add beef or chicken broth

    Add potatoes and bring to boil, cover pot, and lower to medium heat

    Once potatoes have softened, add peas and cook on low for 40 minutes

    Season with salt and pepper

Entrées: Beef

Jane's Beef Bourguignon

Ingredients:

- 3 or 4 pounds boneless beef stew meat cut into cubes about 1½ to 2 inches
- Cooking oil
- 2 cups sliced onions
- ⅔ cups sliced carrots
- 2 cups sliced mushrooms
- 5 to 6 cups red wine
- Beef stock as needed
- 2 or 3 smashed cloves garlic
- 2 cups tomatoes
- 1 bay leaf
- 1 teaspoon thyme
- Salt and pepper to taste
- Beurre Manié Sauce: 3 Tablespoons flour and 3 Tablespoons softened butter blended to a paste.

Directions:

1. In a zip-lock bag place meat, flour, salt, and pepper. Shake up until meat is coated. Meat should be dry, as wet meat and flour make a sticky mess.
2. In large frying pan over medium high heat sauté meat, browning and turning for 3 to 5 minutes. You will have to do more then one batch. Remove meat and place in soup pot.
3. Add prepared vegetables to frying pan and brown slightly. Place them in the soup pot.
4. Pour a cup of the liquid into the frying pan, swishing and scraping up any coagulated juices. Add a traditional Beurre Manié sauce to stew for a richer flavor (use equal parts butter and flour in a saucepan). Add to soup pot.
5. Add the garlic and 4 more cups of liquid into the soup pot. Add tomatoes, bay leaf, thyme, salt, and pepper. You should have enough liquid to almost cover the beef. Add additional beef broth if necessary.
6. Bring to a simmer and cook for 2½ to 3 hours, turning and basting the meat several times until just fork-tender

Chef Note:

- Too much trouble? Just throw everything into the pot for Beef Stew and cook for the same amount of time. You can add carrots, parsnips, potatoes, cabbage or whatever is in your fridge. I would use just beef and/or a tomato broth blend on this and not include the wine.
- The Bourguignon is a great one for a dinner party because it is better the next day. Just make sure to heat it up slowly. To make it a true peasant food dish, you can serve with mashed potatoes or noodles. French Bread and a Cab sound good to me.

Beef Tenderloin Roast

Use a sharp boning knife to trim whole Tenderloin. First remove a narrow strip of meat that is only loosely attached to the main loin, this is known as the "chain". Next trim the excess fat and silver skin from Tenderloin. The large center part makes a great Chateaubriand roast for two. The loin can also be cut into steaks or roasted whole.

Filet Mignon

1. Cut loin into 1½-inch wide steaks filets
2. Coat filets with kosher salt and lemon pepper. Let steak sit at room temp for 30 minutes
3. Grill steaks or Fry by heating pan on high, add butter and some olive oil to prevent smoking in the frying pan.
4. Cook steaks for 4 minutes on each side. Add your favorite steak sauce at the end of the cooking process. Remove and let steaks rest
5. When pan frying, pour off fat from pan, add brandy to deglaze pan, scrape steak bits from pan, turn off stove, use lighter to flash alcohol.
6. This yields a dark glaze, add some cream and heat to make sauce and serve as a side

Chateaubriand

1. Coat roast with olive oil, cover all sides with course salt & lemon pepper seasoning
2. Let rest for 1 hours at room temperature
3. Use cast Iron roasting pan, ideally with raised grill ridges
4. Heat roasting pan on high heat for 8 minutes.
5. Add roast and sear on all sides approx. 8 minutes
6. Let Roast stand for 10 minutes to cool down. Cover with steak sauce
7. Set oven at 250° F, add probe thermometer and cook to 125° F internal steak temp
8. Remove from oven and cover in aluminum foil and let sit for 30 minutes.
9. Make a side sauce by sauté diced shallots in butter, scrape up pan bits add cup of wine and can of beef consommé; reduce mixture in half.
10. Ready for carving

continued on next page

continued from previous page

Tenderloin Roast

1. Slice tenderloin lengthwise to butterfly roast
2. Add salt, lemon pepper, and olive oil
3. Sear on both sides, let cool for 15 minutes
4. Add steak sauce and blue cheese in center and butcher tie roast back together
5. Place in 450° F oven till center reaches 125° F
6. Cover with foil and let rest for 15 minutes
7. Ready for carving

Steak Sandwich

1. Take Tenderloin side chain and remove excess fat
2. Pound out steak chunks with meat mallet
3. In a hot fry pan, add olive oil, steak chunks and season with kosher salt, lemon pepper, and steak sauce. Cook for no more then 8 minutes; set cooked steak and juices aside
4. Julienne a sweet onion, add butter and olive oil, and sauté in fry pan
5. Chop up steak and add to steak bun with cheddar cheese and cooked onions
6. Enjoy your "Philly-style" steak sandwich

Beef Wellington

Ingredients:

    4 beef tenderloin steak filets

    1 cup chopped onions

    1 cup chopped mushrooms

    2 minced cloves garlic

    2 Tablespoons butter

    2 cups cooking sherry

    2 full sheets puff pastry

    Dijon mustard

    Salt and pepper

    Egg wash

Directions:

1. Bring filets to room temperature, season with salt and pepper
2. Bring skillet to high heat
3. Sear all sides and edges of filets, and set filets aside
4. Add butter, chopped onions, mushrooms, and garlic to skillet, and stir for 2 minutes
5. Cover vegetables with cooking sherry, add salt and pepper and reduce to a soft filling paste
6. Lay down sheet of plastic wrap and place ½ piece of pastry dough on top
7. Add spoonful of filling onto center of dough.
8. Spread Dijon mustard on filet and put filet on top of filling, then add another spoonful of filling on top of filet.
9. Fold pastry around filet and use plastic film to squeeze and roll pastry dough to seal edges. Remove plastic film.
10. Place on cooking sheet and egg wash pastry top and side.
11. Preheat oven to 425° F and cook for 25 minutes

Jason Kretchman's Grilled Asian Flank Steak

Ingredients:

    tortillas, or leaf lettuce wrap

    1 pkg cole slaw

Marinade:

    ¼ cup light soy sauce

    ¼ cup light teriyaki sauce

    3 Tablespoons rice wine vinegar

    2 Tablespoons Asian garlic-chili sauce

    1 Tablespoons minced, fresh ginger

    5 to 10 green onions, chopped

    1 to 2 lbs flank steak

Dressing:

    1 Tablespoon fish sauce

    ¼ cup rice wine vinegar

    1 teaspoon dark sesame oil

    2 garlic cloves, minced, or 2 teaspoons garlic seasoning

    ½ teaspoon crushed red pepper flakes

Directions:

1. Combine soy sauce, teriyaki sauce, and next 4 ingredients in a large, plastic freezer bag, or 9 x 13 baking dish
2. Add steak, and turn to coat. Seal, or cover, and chill 4 hours, or overnight, turning occasionally
3. Remove steak from marinade, discarding marinade
4. Grill flank steak on cast iron skillet, or grill, over medium-high heat, 5 to 7 minutes on each side, or to desired degree of doneness.
5. Let stand 10 minutes before slicing. Cut diagonally across the grain into thin strips.
6. Combine dressing ingredients in a bowl and mix.
7. Add cole slaw and toss to coat with dressing.

Mom's Hamburger Bar-B-Q

Ingredients:

- 2 lbs. hamburger meat
- 4 Tablespoons brown sugar
- 4 Tablespoons mustard
- 4 Tablespoons vinegar
- 3 Tablespoons Worcestershire sauce
- ½ cup ketchup
- 4 Tablespoons sweet pickle relish

Directions:

1. In a hot skillet, cook hamburger until done. Stir frequently to break up into pieces
2. Drain excess fat from cooked hamburger
3. Add remaining ingredients and stir over low heat to combine
4. Let simmer for 15 minutes

Serve with hamburger buns, potato chips, sweet pickle relish, whole or sliced pickles.

Bacon-Wrapped Meatloaf

Ingredients:

3 Tablespoons extra-virgin olive oil

1 large sweet onion, peeled and diced

1 sweet red pepper, cored, seeds removed, and diced

2 cloves garlic, peeled and minced

2 tomatoes, seeded, and finely chopped

¼ cup chopped fresh parsley

12 oz. ketchup

1 Tablespoon Worcestershire sauce

4 slices white bread, crusts removed and torn into pieces

½ cup heavy cream or whole milk

1 pound ground beef

1 pound ground pork

1 cup graded cheddar cheese

1 egg

leaves from 2 fresh thyme sprigs

¾ pound sliced smoked bacon

Salt and pepper

continued on next page

continued from previous page

Directions:

1. Preheat the oven to 350 F.

2. Coat a skillet with olive oil and place over medium heat. Saute the onion, red pepper, and garlic and cook them for a couple of minutes to soften.

3. Add the tomatoes and stir in the parsley, ketchup, and Worcestershire sauce; season with salt and pepper.

4. Simmer this relish for 10 minutes to pull all the flavors together. Remove it from the heat; you should have about 4 cups of relish.

5. In a large mixing bowl soak the bread pieces in the whole milk. Set aside.

6. In a separate large mixing bowl, combine the ground beef with the ground pork and mix well.

7. Squeeze out the milk from the bread and add the bread to the meat. Add the egg, 1 cup of the tomato relish, cheese, and thyme; season with salt and pepper. Mix well with hands.

8. To test, fry a small "hamburger" patty of the meatloaf until cooked; the patty should hold together but still have a soft consistency. Taste the patty for seasoning.

9. Line a baking tray with parchment paper. Form the meat into a loaf shape on the tray

10. Cover the shaped loaf with slices of bacon.

11. Bake the meatloaf for 1 to 1½ hours until the juices run clear and meat is tender — it should spring back lightly when pressed. A meat thermometer should show an internal temp of 165°F

12. Remove the meatloaf from the oven and let it rest for 10 minutes before slicing between the bacon slices. Serve with the remaining tomato relish on the side.

Pot Roast

Ingredients:

4 pounds boneless beef chuck roast, tied (ask your butcher to do this)
Kosher salt and freshly-cracked black pepper
¼ cup canola oil
½ cup all-purpose flour
2 carrots, peeled and cut into large chunks
2 turnips, peeled and cut into large chunks
1 red onion, cut into large chunks
2 Tablespoons tomato paste
5 cloves garlic, peeled
3 sprigs fresh thyme
2 bay leaves
2 12-ounce bottles stout beer
2 cups beef stock
4 Tablespoons butter
2 cups frozen pearl onions
2 cups frozen green peas
¼ cup thinly sliced chives

continued on next page

continued from previous page

Directions:

1. The night before, season the chuck roast liberally with salt and pepper and refrigerate uncovered.

2. When ready to cook, preheat the oven to 300° F.

3. In a large Dutch oven, heat the canola oil over medium-high heat. Season the chuck roast again with salt and pepper and dust with flour, shaking off the excess. Sear on all sides, browning the meat evenly, 4 to 6 minutes per side. Remove the roast to a plate, and then add the carrots, turnips and onion to the pot. Lower the heat to medium and cook, stirring occasionally, until the vegetables are caramelized, 6 to 8 minutes. Stir in the tomato paste, garlic, thyme and bay leaves and cook another 2 minutes.

4. Add the roast back to the pot, and then add the beer and beef stock. Nestle the roast down among the vegetables so that it is mostly submerged in the liquid. Bring to a simmer. Cover, leaving the lid slightly ajar, and place in the oven to cook until very tender, 3 to 3½ hours, testing with a small knife for tenderness after 3 hours.

5. Meanwhile, heat the butter in saucepot over medium-low heat; add the pearl onions and peas and season with salt and pepper. Cook, stirring occasionally, until the onions and peas are warmed through, 3 to 5 minutes.

6. Once the roast is done, remove it from the pot and cut off the string. Discard the thyme and bay leaves. If you'd like the sauce thicker, place the Dutch oven back on the stove and bring to a simmer over medium-high heat. Simmer, stirring occasionally, until the liquid is reduced to the desired thickness (you're looking for a rich and smooth sauce).

7. To plate, slice the roast into thick slices. Place the vegetables on a platter, then the sliced beef, and then ladle the sauce over. Spoon the peas and onions on top and sprinkle with the chives.

Standing Rib Roast (Prime Rib Roast)

Ingredients:

    8-lb. prime rib roast (3-bone roast). Take roast out of packaging and refrigerate uncovered on a rimmed platter to dry age for 24 hours before marinating or cooking

Marinade (it is optional to marinate roast — recipe works well without marinating):

    4 cups beef stock or canned broth, wine, or beer. I would use a combo of beer and beef stock

    ⅓ cup orange marmalade

    4 cloves garlic, chopped

    1 shallot, peeled and chopped

    3 Tablespoons Worcestershire sauce or your favorite steak sauce

    4 Tablespoons brown sugar

Roasting Sauce:

    ½ cup Dijon mustard

    ¼ cup your favorite steak sauce

    2 Tablespoons your favorite fresh chopped herbs (sage, thyme)

Season Roast:

    ¼ cup extra-virgin olive oil

    coarse sea or kosher salt

    freshly ground pepper

    3 to 4 cloves garlic, sliced lengthwise

Jus:

    2 Tablespoons butter

    1 cup beer or wine

    parsley for garnishing

Horseradish Sauce (optional):

    1 cup sour cream

    3 to 4 Tablespoons prepared horseradish

    1 teaspoon coarsely ground pepper

    ⅛ teaspoon Worcestershire sauce or your favorite steak sauce

continued on next page

continued from previous page

Directions:

For Marinating:

1. Combine beef stock, chopped garlic, shallot, orange Marmalade, Worcestershire sauce, and brown sugar. Warm to dissolve into solution. Cool

2. Cut lightly into roast surface and fat with a sharp knife

3. Pour marinade over roast. Cover and chill for at least 6 hours. A marinating bag works best, so you can flip to proportionately coat roast

Cooking:

1. Remove roast from the refrigerator 2 hours before cooking. Thoroughly pat the roast dry with paper towels and let rest to reach room temperature

2. Place oven rack in the lower third of the oven and preheat oven to 500* F

3. Place roast fat side up in a large, deep baking pan with a roasting rack

4. Coat all sides of the roast with olive oil and sprinkle liberally with coarse sea or kosher salt and ground back pepper. Use paring knife to cut ¾-inch deep hole in the top (fat) side and insert sliced garlic at 1½ inch spacing from each other

5. Thoroughly mix Dijon mustard and favorite steak sauce in bowl. Cover top fat side of roast with this mixture

6. Ideally, insert a roasting thermometer with a cable and external readout into the middle of the roast, making sure the thermometer does not touch any bone. The thermometer readout will be placed outside the oven

7. Place roast in preheated 500° F oven for one hour. **Then turn off the oven, but do not open the oven door at any time**

8. Allow the roast to continue to cook in the closed oven for about 2 hours or until the meat thermometer reading is 118° F for rare, 140° F for medium-rare, and 170° F for well done

9. Transfer to platter, re-tent with aluminum foil, and let rest for 20 minutes, while you prepare the jus

10. Pour off all fat from roasting pan

11. Place pan over medium-high heat and add in some wine or beer, bringing to a boil

12. Scrape up any browned bits from roasting pan add 2 Tablespoons butter and season to taste. Add a Tablespoon of your favorite steak sauce for taste

13. Pour jus into sauce bowl and garnish platter with parsley.

Some guests enjoy their Prime Rib with a serving of Horseradish Sauce (mix ingredients in list together)

Esther Gallagher's Steak Stroganoff

This is a great slow cooker recipe that we've served many times. We have even packed our slow cooker as we traveled to Hilton Head!! This dish was always appreciated after a day at the ocean.

Makes 6 servings

Ingredients:

- 2 Tablespoons flour
- ½ teaspoon garlic powder
- ½ teaspoon pepper
- ¼ teaspoon paprika
- 1¾ lbs. boneless beef round steak
- 10¾ oz. can cream of mushroom soup
- ½ cup water
- 1 envelope dried onion soup mix
- 9-oz. jar sliced mushrooms, drained
- ½ cup sour cream
- 1 Tablespoon minced fresh parsley

Directions:

1. Combine flour, garlic powder, pepper, and paprika in slow cooker
2. Cut meat into 1½ x ½-inch strips. Place in flour mixture and toss until meat is well coated
3. Add mushroom soup, water, and soup mix. Stir until well blended
4. Cover and cook on high 3 to 3½ hours, or low for 6 to 7 hours
5. Stir in mushrooms, sour cream, and parsley. Cover and cook on high 10 to 15 minutes, or until heated through

Serve with rice or egg noodles

Veal Liver and Onions

Serves 2

Ingredients:

- 1 lb. veal (aka baby beef) liver, sliced
- 4 slices bacon, thick sliced preferred
- 1 medium sweet onion, sliced
- ¼ cup butter, **not** margarine
- 1 Tablespoon flour
- Merlot or Marsala wine

Directions:

1. In cold water, drain and rinse liver of all blood. Pat liver dry
2. Slice bacon in half and lightly brown in a heavy skillet (cast iron is best)
3. Add the sliced onion and cook until lightly brown, making sure that the bacon doesn't get too crisp
4. Remove bacon and onion from skillet; set aside and keep warm, discarding excess bacon grease
5. Melt the butter in skillet with residual bacon grease
6. Sprinkle flour on liver and place in skillet
7. Brown both sides being careful not to overcook
8. Just cover liver with Merlot or Marsala wine and cover pan and cook to reduce liquid in half. Flip liver slices and stir wine sauce once during final cook

Remove to warm plates/platter and top with bacon/onion mixture

See Crispy Smashed Potato recipe to make a great side

Entrées: Fish and Seafood

Jane's Coquilles Saint-Jacques

I first made this recipe with Sharon in the early 70's. This dish has a great WOW factor in serving to your dinner guests. This recipe is traditionally served on scallop shells, but ovenproof ramekins are an ok substitution.

Ingredients:

Poached Scallops:

- 1½ lbs. scallops — if they are large you may want to cut them in half
- 1½ Tablespoons minced shallots or scallions
- ⅔ cups dry white wine or vermouth
- ½ cup water, or more if needed
- 1 bay leaf
- ½ teaspoon salt

Velouté Sauce:

- 3 Tablespoons butter
- 3 Tablespoons flour
- 3 droplets freshly-squeezed lemon juice
- Salt and freshly-ground pepper to taste
- ¾ cup heavy cream
- Milk, as needed
- 1 cup grated Swiss cheese (I might use Gruyère)

continued on next page

continued from previous page

Directions:

Poach the Scallops:

1. Simmer the wine, water, bay leaf and salt for 3 minutes.

2. Add the scallops. The liquid should almost cover the scallops; add more water, if needed. Hold the temperature at simmer for about 1½ to 2 minutes, or until the scallops are lightly springy rather than squishy to the touch.

3. Remove the scallops to a bowl, discard the bay leaf, and boil down the poaching liquid to 1 cup. Save the reduced poaching liquid for your sauce.

Prepare the Veloute Sauce and Assemble:

1. Butter the scallop shells or ramekins. Arrange shells on cookie sheet. If the shells are unsteady, you can use crumbled aluminum foil so the shells don't slide and tip over.

2. Melt the butter and combine with the flour and lemon juice for 2 minutes.

3. Take off the heat and beat in the hot poaching liquid and heavy cream.

4. Season sauce and simmer 3 minutes, adding droplets of milk if the sauce is too thick.

5. Place scallops in the shells.

6. Fold enough of the sauce over the scallops to cover them, and then top each with the grated cheese.

7. Just before you are ready to serve this dish, place the cookie sheet with your loaded shells 4 inches below your broiler element. Broil until bubbling hot and the cheese is melted.

Chef Note:

- Everything through step 6 can be done ahead of time and refrigerated.

Grandma Ida Gallagher Mumford's Crab Cakes

by Grandson Eddie Gallagher

When Eddie was in the 9th grade, he would help Grandma Mumford clean her house and help her cook. There was a Fire Hall that had a bar. Grandma decided to made a deal with the Fire Hall! Every weekend Grandma Ida would cook her crab cakes, pepper cabbage, stuffing, and turkey. There was a sell-out crowd each week. She had a booming business!

Ingredients:

- 1 lb. crabmeat
- 8 eggs, hard boiled and mashed
- ¼ cup onion, chopped
- 1 cup Miracle Whip™
- 1 cup bread crumbs
- dash of cayenne pepper
- 2 eggs, beaten with ¼ cup milk for Bowl #1
- cracker crumbs for coating for Bowl #2
- bread crumbs for coating for Bowl #3

Directions:

1. Mix first 6 ingredients thoroughly. Use about ⅓ cup of mixture for each patty
2. Once the patties are made you will need to set up the 3-step coating process:
    a. First, dip patties in egg mixture, then dip in cracker crumbs. Place patties on baking sheet lined with wax paper
    b. Second, dip patties back into egg mixture, then dip in bread crumbs
    c. Finally, dip in egg mixture again, then dip in bread crumbs again
3. Heat about 2 to 3 Tablespoons olive oil in large pan over medium heat
4. Once hot, add crab cakes and cook for about 3 to 4 minutes on one side until golden brown on bottom
5. Gently flip to other side for another 3 minutes or until golden brown

Serve with tartar sauce

Deb's Baked Scallops

Ingredients:

    2 lbs. sea scallops

    Salt and pepper

    1 teaspoon fresh thyme, minced

    ½ cup buttermilk

    2 cups hand crushed Ritz™ crackers

    ½ cup butter, melted

    1 small lemon, halved

Directions:

1. Preheat oven to 400° F
2. Place scallops in a bowl, season with salt and pepper, add thyme and buttermilk, and toss to coat
3. Place scallops, with buttermilk, evenly in the bottom of an ovenproof dish, sprinkle with cracker crumbs and top with melted butter
4. Bake for 20 minutes
5. Squeeze lemon over scallops and serve immediately

Carolina Low-Country Shrimp and Sausage Boil

Shana Westley Young requested this for her High School Graduation Party

Serves 4

Ingredients:
- 1 pound baby red potatoes or baby yellow potatoes, washed
- 1 pound shrimp, peeled and deveined
- 1 pound smoked sausage, chopped in 1-inch pieces
- 2 ears corn-on-the-cob, husked and cut into thirds
- 1 sweet onion, chopped
- 3 Tablespoons Old Bay™ seasoning or homemade seasoning (see note)
- Salt and pepper, to taste
- 1 Tablespoon minced garlic
- Juice of ½ lemon, plus lemon wedges for serving
- 3 Tablespoons butter melted + ½ cup, divided
- Chopped fresh parsley, for topping

Directions:
1. Chop potatoes into 2 inch pieces
2. Boil potatoes in salted water for 10 minutes. Drain and place in large bowl
3. Add and combine shrimp, sausage, corn, and onion with the potatoes
4. Melt 3 Tablespoons butter, add Old Bay™ seasoning, garlic, juice from half a lemon, and salt and pepper to taste. Pour this mixture over shrimp, sausage, and veggies. Stir to coat
5. Divide between four 12 x 12 inch sheets of aluminum foil. Fold edges of foil up around the food to create a closed packet
6. Cook on preheated grill over medium-high heat for 8 to 10 minutes on one side, then flip and cook another 5 to 6 minutes on the second side. Alternately, you can bake the packets in the oven at 400° F for 15 to 20 minutes until corn is tender and shrimp are pink and fully cooked
7. While packets are cooking, melt remaining butter in a medium saucepan over medium-high heat. Once melted, continue to stir gently over medium heat for 3 to 4 minutes longer until color changes from pale yellow to a golden amber (but be careful not to burn it)
8. Serve shrimp boil packs topped with chopped parsley and lemon wedges for garnish

Recipe Notes:
- An outdoor deep fryer Boil is the traditional fun way to do this recipe. This recipe was adjusted to take into account that most people do not have an outdoor deep fryer.
- Live Crawfish are a great substitute/addition for Shrimp in an outside Boil.
- For Homemade Old Bay™ Seasoning: whisk together 1 Tablespoon celery salt, 1 teaspoon paprika, ½ teaspoon black pepper, ½ teaspoon cayenne pepper, ¼ teaspoon dry mustard, ⅛ teaspoon each allspice, cloves, and a pinch of ground ginger.

Jane's Pineapple Shrimp Boat

My Signature Dish

Serves 4

Ingredients:
- Fruit Salsa:
  - 2 whole ripe pineapples
  - 1 Tablespoon minced fresh mint leaves
  - 1 Tablespoon minced ginger
  - ¼ cup rice vinegar
  - 1 pinch red pepper flakes
  - ¾ cup small diced red onion
  - 1 cup small diced red bell pepper
  - 15-ounce can apricots, drained and diced
- Shrimp:
  - 2 pounds (21 / 25 count) shrimp, cleaned and deveined
  - ⅓ cup soy sauce
  - 1 Tablespoon minced lemongrass
  - 2 Tablespoons minced ginger
  - 2 Tablespoons cornstarch
  - 2 Tablespoons peanut oil
  - 2 cups diced red bell pepper
  - 2 cups diced yellow onion
  - 1 Tablespoon minced jalapeno
  - 1 Tablespoon minced garlic

Directions:

Fruit Salsa: Ideal to make the day before and let flavors combine.

1. Halve the whole pineapples trying to leave some of the top leaves with each half. Remove the pineapple core and fruit meat, creating 4 small boats for serving. Remove the pineapple core from the fruit and dice the fruit.
2. In a glass bowl, combine the mint, ginger, rice vinegar, and red pepper flakes. Stir in the pineapple, the onions, red bell pepper, and apricots. Cover and refrigerate for at least 30 minutes before final combination.

Make Drunken Coconut Rice - see recipe on page 173

Shrimp:

3. In a re-sealable plastic bag, add the shrimp, 3 Tablespoons soy sauce, the lemongrass, 1 Tablespoon of ginger and the cornstarch and combine well. Refrigerate for 30 minutes.
4. In a large sauté pan over high heat, heat the peanut oil and add half the shrimp mixture. Sauté for 3 to 4 minutes and remove. Repeat for second batch of shrimp, adding additional oil, if necessary.
5. Add the diced red bell pepper and diced onion to the pan and sauté for 3 minutes. Stir in the jalapeno, garlic, and the remaining Tablespoon of ginger and remaining soy sauce. Add the shrimp back into the sauté pan and heat until warmed through.

Serving a tremendous Dinner Presentation:

Add Drunken Coconut Rice as the first layer inside the pineapple shells; Then add a second layer of cold Salsa; then add a third layer of the shrimp mixture; and top it off with more cold Salsa for serving.

Lisa's Shrimp Scampi

Ingredients:

    2 pounds shrimp, peeled and cleaned

    ⅓ cup oil

    2 small garlic cloves, minced

    1 teaspoon salt

    ½ teaspoon pepper

    ¼ cup fresh lemon juice

Directions:

1. Heat oil in large skillet
2. Stir in garlic, salt, pepper, and lemon juice
3. Add shrimp
4. Cook until shrimp turns pink
5. Reduce heat and cook until liquid is almost absorbed. Do not overcook shrimp

Serve hot

Baked Lemon Butter Shrimp

Easy and Lemony!

This baked shrimp makes the perfect side dish, or you can have it as a main dish with some salad aside!

Ingredients:

- 1 lb. raw shrimp, cleaned, peeled, and deveined
- 8 Tablespoons melted butter
- 3 cloves minced garlic
- 1 packet Italian all-natural seasoning
- 1½ lemons, sliced into thin circles
- 1 Tablespoon dried parsley leaves
- 1 Tablespoon ground black pepper

Directions:

1. Sauté and pour the mixture of the melted butter and minced garlic into a 9 x 11-inch glass casserole dish
2. Place the lemon slices over the butter then top with a layer of the shrimp
3. Season by sprinkling with the Italian seasoning, parsley flakes, and pepper on top
4. Preheat oven to 350°F bake for 15 minutes

Sharon's Spicy Shrimp

Ingredients:

- 2 pounds large shrimp. I buy the pre-cooked shrimp with tails on. Adjust quantity based on number of guests
- ¼ cup good quality virgin olive oil
- 1 Tablespoon finely minced garlic
- 1 Tablespoon finely minced shallots
- 2 Tablespoons lemon juice or more to taste
- 2 sweet peppers (recommend one red and one orange)
- 2 Tablespoons chopped fresh dill
- Baguette of French bread

Directions:

1. Combine the olive oil, minced garlic, minced shallots, and lemon juice to make a marinade
2. Place all the cooked shrimp and marinade in a large zip-lock bag. Place in refrigerator. Turn the bag frequently so that the marinade continues to contact all of the shrimp. Refrigerate for a minimum of 3 to 4 hours
3. Drain the marinade and adjust the seasonings to taste
4. Place shrimp on a large serving platter
5. Remove the seeds from the red and orange peppers and slice them into strips for placing on the sides of platter. Cover the shrimp with the chopped fresh dill

Serve sliced French bread in a basket next to shrimp

Can be served as a first course or as an appetizer on long bamboo skewers

Can also be served with pasta

Entrées: Irish Specialties

Corned Beef and Cabbage

Preparation time: 35 minutes
Baking time: 3 hours
Yield: 8 servings

Ingredients:

    3 to 3½-pound corned beef brisket

Seasoning:

    1 cup apple cider or apple juice

    1 teaspoon whole black peppercorns

    2 bay leaves

Vegetables:

    10 small, whole, white onions, about 1 pound

    4 medium potatoes, peeled, cut into quarters

    1 medium rutabaga, peeled, cut into 2-inch chunks, about 4 cups

    1 head cabbage, cut into 8 wedges, center core, root, and outside leaves removed

Mustard Sauce:

    1 cup Heavy Whipping Cream

    ¼ cup Dijon mustard

    ¼ cup prepared horseradish

    2 Tablespoons balsamic vinegar or red wine vinegar

Directions:

1. Heat oven to 325° F. Place beef brisket in roaster; add juices and spices from brisket package. Combine all seasoning ingredients in small bowl; pour over brisket. Cover and bake for 2 hours

2. Add vegetables. Cover and continue baking for 1 to 1½ hours or until brisket is fork tender and vegetables are desired doneness. Remove brisket and vegetables to serving platter; keep warm

3. Beat whipping cream in chilled small bowl at high speed until soft peaks form. Gently stir in horseradish, mustard, and vinegar by hand. Serve mustard sauce with brisket and vegetables. Cover; store refrigerated up to three days. This mustard sauce is also good served with roast beef and pork

Irish Stew

Yield: 6 1⅓-cup servings

Ingredients:

    2 Tablespoons butter

    1 pound beef stew meat, cut into 1-inch cubes

    1½ teaspoons salt

    ½ teaspoon pepper

    1 pound (3 cups) potatoes, peeled, cut into 1-inch cubes

    1 large (1½ cups) onion, coarsely chopped

    2 medium (1 cup) carrots, peeled, sliced into 1-inch rounds

    1 leek, cut in half lengthwise, then cut into ¼-inch slices

    3 cloves finely chopped garlic

    1 cup dark stout beer or apple juice

    1 cup tomato juice

    14½-ounce can beef broth

    1 bay leaf

    1 Tablespoon sugar

    1 Tablespoon Worcestershire sauce

    1 teaspoon dried thyme leaves

Directions:

1. Melt 1 Tablespoon butter in 4-quart saucepan over medium-high heat. Add stew meat; sprinkle with ½ teaspoon salt and ¼ teaspoon pepper. Cook, stirring occasionally, until browned (5 to 7 minutes). Remove meat to plate and set aside

2. Melt remaining Tablespoon of butter in same pan; add potatoes, onion, carrots, leek, garlic, beer, tomato juice, and beef broth. Cook, stirring occasionally, until vegetables start to soften (5 to 7 minutes)

3. Return meat to pan; add 1 teaspoon salt, ¼ teaspoon pepper, and all remaining ingredients. Continue cooking until stew comes to a boil (5 to 6 minutes)

4. Reduce heat to low. Cover and cook until beef is tender (1½ to 2 hours)

Shepherd's Pie

Excellent dish when you have leftover mashed potatoes

Ingredients:

- 2 lbs hamburger
- 1 can beef gravy
- 8 oz. each frozen corn, peas and mixed vegetables, thawed (can be mixed according to individual's preference)
- 1 sweet onion, chopped
- 1 sweet pepper, chopped
- 4 lbs. potatoes or leftover mashed potatoes
- 1 whole scallion washed and finely chopped
- sour cream and whole milk
- grated cheddar cheese
- salt and pepper to taste

Directions:

1. Peel and cube the potatoes and boil in salted water until tender
2. While the potatoes are cooking, cook the hamburger until brown, drain the excess fat, and set aside
3. Add some butter to the hamburger pan and sauté the chopped peppers and onions until translucent
4. After the potatoes are tender, drain them and add chopped scallion, 4 pats of butter, and, using a potato masher, add just enough milk and sour cream equally to get a firm mashed potato mixture
5. In a large casserole dish mix thoroughly the hamburger, thawed vegetables, sautéed onions and peppers, and beef gravy
6. Cover this mixture with the mashed potatoes
7. Add grated cheese and a couple of pats of butter on top of the mashed potatoes
8. Bake approximately 45 minutes in a 375° F oven

Entrées: Italian Specialties

Angel Hair Pasta With Lemon and White Beans

This is an old Weight Watcher™ recipe that is a nice change from a red tomato sauce. Now with WW Freestyle™ points, the cannellini beans are 0 points — but you still have to count the pasta for points!

by Esther Gallagher

Serves 6

Ingredients:

　　Zest of 1 lemon, finely grated

　　¼ cup fresh lemon juice

　　2 Tablespoons margarine

　　2 Tablespoons olive oil

　　¼ teaspoon freshly ground pepper

　　3 cups chicken broth

　　15½-oz. can cannellini beans

　　½ cup chopped basil

　　¼ cup chopped parsley

　　12 oz. angel hair pasta, cooked and drained

　　Grated Parmesan cheese

Directions:

1. In medium serving bowl, combine lemon zest, lemon juice, margarine, olive oil, and pepper. Set aside.

2. In large saucepan, heat broth* and add beans, basil, and parsley. Cook stirring frequently, 2 to 3 minutes, until heated through.

3. Add pasta to serving bowl and toss lightly. Add bean mixture and toss to mix well.

4. Sprinkle with grated cheese.

*HINT: I lightly thicken the sauce with about 1 Tablespoon cornstarch to 2 Tablespoons cold water before adding the beans, basil and parsley.

Chicken Cacciatore

In 1984, our "civic minded" mother was one of the founding members of the Italian American Women's Assn. In 2009, the ladies compiled a cookbook for their 25th Anniversary. My sister Dolores and I submitted some of her best recipes. Chicken Cacciatore was one of them.

In 1968, when Ed's mom, Joyce, along with Debbie and Lisa drove to Erie to meet my family Chicken Cacciatore was on the menu for their welcome dinner.

Ingredients:
- About 5 lbs. cut up chicken pieces
- Flour for dredging
- Salt and pepper to taste
- ¼ cup vegetable oil
- ¼ cup olive oil
- 1 lb. 12 oz. can crushed tomatoes
- ½ teaspoon salt
- ¼ teaspoon pepper
- ¼ teaspoon dried basil
- ½ to ¾ cup Marsala or sherry wine
- 1 cup coarsely chopped onions
- 1 cup red pepper, cut into ½ inch chunks
- 1 cup green or yellow peppers, cut into ½ inch chunks
- 2 cups sliced mushrooms

Directions:
1. Season the chicken pieces generously with salt and pepper. Dredge the pieces in flour, coating them lightly and tapping off the excess flour. Brown the chicken in the oil. Do not crowd the chicken, cook in batches if necessary. Remove the browned chicken to a roasting pan and sprinkle each piece with sherry or Marsala wine. Keep in a warm oven until all the chicken is cooked.
2. Simmer the crushed tomatoes, salt, pepper, basil and Marsala/sherry for about ½ hour
3. Saute onions, red pepper, green/yellow peppers, and mushrooms in the olive oil
4. Spread the vegetable mixture over the chicken pieces and pour the tomato sauce over chicken and vegetables, bake in a 350°F oven for about 40 to 45 minutes or until chicken is tender.

Esther Gallagher's Eggplant Parmigiana

Serves 6 to 8

Ingredients:

¾ cup flour

2 teaspoons salt

2 eggs, beaten

1 large eggplant, cut into ¼-inch slices

Olive oil

Your favorite Marinara sauce

½ cup Parmesan cheese

12 - 14 oz. Mozzarella cheese, cut into stripes

Directions:

1. On a sheet of waxed paper, combine flour and salt. Dip eggplant into beaten eggs, then coat with flour mixture. Heat oil in a large skillet over medium heat. Cook eggplant a few slices at a time until golden, adding oil as needed. Remove from skillet and drain on a paper towel.

2. Spoon some sauce into a greased 13 x 9-inch baking pan. Arrange half the eggplant slices in pan and sprinkle with Parmesan cheese. Spread half the tomato sauce over eggplant along with half the Mozzarella strips.

3. Repeat layers, ending with sauce. Bake in a 350° F oven for 40 - 45 minutes or until bubbly. Ten minutes before serving, add remainder of Mozzarella strips and cook until cheese has melted.

Chef Note:

- Another variation of this casserole is to sauté 2 Tablespoons chopped onions in 2 Tablespoons olive oil until onions are lightly golden. Add 1 pound ground beef and cook until meat is brown, stirring to break up the meat into small pieces. Season with salt and pepper. Drain off fat and set mixture aside. When you begin layering the casserole, add this mixture on top of the eggplant layers.

Lasagna

Ingredients:

Meat Mixture:

¾ pound ground round

Vegetable cooking spray

1 cup chopped onion

3 garlic cloves, minced

¼ cup chopped fresh parsley, divided

Tomato Mixture:

28-ounce can whole tomatoes, undrained and chopped

14½-ounce can Italian-style stewed tomatoes, undrained and chopped

8-ounce can no-salt-added tomato sauce

6-ounce can tomato paste

2 teaspoons dried oregano

1 teaspoon dried basil

¼ teaspoon pepper

Cheese Mixture:

2 cups grated Mozzarella cheese

½ cup (1 ounce) finely grated fresh Parmesan cheese

15-ounce container nonfat ricotta cheese

1 egg white, lightly beaten

Assemble:

12 cooked lasagna noodles

2 cups (8 ounces) shredded Italian provolone cheese

Fresh oregano sprigs (optional)

continued on next page

continued from previous page

Directions:

1. Boil 12 Lasagna noodles in salt water till soft

2. Cook meat in a large saucepan over medium heat until browned, stirring to crumble; drain fat and set aside.

3. Wipe pan with a paper towel. Coat pan with cooking spray; add the onion and garlic, and sauté 5 minutes.

4. Return meat to pan. Add 2 Tablespoons parsley and next 7 tomato mixture ingredients; bring to a boil. Cover, reduce heat, and simmer 15 minutes. Uncover; simmer 20 minutes. Remove from heat.

5. Combine remaining 2 Tablespoons parsley, mozzarella cheese, and next 3 ingredients in a bowl; stir well, and set aside.

6. Coat a 13 x 9-inch baking dish with cooking spray and spread a light layer of tomato mixture in bottom of the dish.

7. Arrange 4 noodles over tomato mixture; top with half of cheese mixture, one third of the tomato mixture, and one third of the provolone.

8. Repeat layers, ending with noodles. Spread the remaining tomato mixture over noodles.

9. Cover and bake at 350° F for 1 hour.

10. Sprinkle with remaining provolone; bake, uncovered, for 10 minutes.

    Let stand 10 minutes before serving.

    Garnish with oregano, if desired.

Esther Gallagher's Linguine With White Clam Sauce

This was my mother's original recipe! It was the "Friday Special" served in our restaurant. Every Friday customers would line up outside the restaurant to enjoy a plate ot Linguine or the other "Friday Special," Lake Erie Perch Dinner.

Serves 4-6

Ingredients:

- ⅓ cup olive oil
- 2 cloves garlic, chopped
- ⅓ cup onions, chopped
- ½ stick butter
- 4 6½-oz. cans chopped clams, drained, reserve juice
- 8-oz. bottle clam juice
- Salt and pepper to taste
- Crushed red pepper flakes, to taste
- ½ cup parsley, chopped
- 1 lb. linguine
- Grated Parmesan cheese

Directions:

1. In saucepan, sauté onions and garlic in olive oil until lightly golden. Add butter and stir until melted
2. Add reserved clam juice and bottled juice to above mixture . Season with salt and pepper to taste. Simmer for ½ hour
3. Thicken sauce lightly using 2 to 3 Tablespoons corn starch to about ¼ cup cold water
4. Add chopped clams, red pepper flakes and 2 Tablespoons chopped parsley
5. Cook linguine, *al dente*. Drain. Place linguine on platter. Sprinkle with remaining parsley. Add Parmesan cheese. Add clam sauce and serve

Marinara Sauce

by Esther Gallagher via Angie DiTullio

Ingredients:

- ½ cup olive oil
- 1 Tablespoons chopped garlic
- 2 Tablespoons chopped onions
- 1 lb. 12-oz. can crushed tomatoes
- 2 fresh basil leaves or ¼ teaspoon dried basil
- ½ teaspoon salt
- ¼ teaspoon pepper

Directions:

1. In a saucepan heat oil and sauté onions until lightly golden; add garlic and sauté until golden in color.
2. Mash tomatoes until tomato pieces are small. Add tomatoes to garlic and onion mixture. Add basil, salt and pepper. Simmer for 1 hour.

Serve over your favorite pasta.

Peas and Pasta Shells

Here is another vegetarian recipes from my Mom, Angie DiTullio!! Her marinara sauce on the previous page has always been a big hit with everyone. These recipes are simple, quick and "Oh, soooo good!"

by Esther Gallagher via Angie DiTullio

Serves 6

Ingredients:

- 8 oz. medium pasta seashells, boiled and drained
- 2½ cups frozen peas, thawed
- 1 cup onion, finely chopped
- 2 garlic cloves, minced
- ¼ cup olive oil
- ½ cup butter
- 1 cup parsley, finely chopped
- ½ teaspoon salt
- Black pepper to taste
- Parmesan cheese

Directions:

1. Sauté onions and garlic in combined oil and butter for 10 minutes
2. Add cooked pasta shells, peas, parsley, salt, and pepper. Mix well
3. Place in casserole. Cover and bake in 350° F oven for 20 - 25 minutes

Serve with grated Parmesan cheese

Jane and Sharon's Spaghetti Carbonara

Serves 4

Ingredients:

- 6 thick-cut pancetta or bacon slices, chopped
- 2 garlic cloves, minced
- 2 eggs, at room temperature
- 2 egg yolks
- ½ cup plus 2 Tablespoons grated Pecorino Romano cheese
- 1 lb. spaghetti or bucatini noodles
- 2 Tablespoons chopped fresh flat-leaf parsley
- Kosher salt and freshly ground pepper to taste

Directions:

1. Heat a large skillet over medium heat; add oil and the pancetta. Cook, stirring often, until just starting to get crisp, about 6 minutes total. Using a slotted spoon, transfer the pancetta to a large bowl.
2. Remove the pan from the heat and add the garlic to the fat in the pan. Add olive oil if necessary to let the garlic soften in the residual skillet heat, about 30 seconds. Using a slotted spoon, transfer the garlic to the bowl with the bacon.
3. Crack the 2 eggs and 2 yolks into a small bowl. Beat and stir in the ½ cup grated Pecorino Romano cheese. Set aside.
4. Bring a large pot of generously salted water to a boil over high heat. Add the spaghetti and cook according to the package directions.
5. Drain the pasta, reserving ½ cup of the pasta cooking water to adjust the sauce.
6. Add the pasta to the bowl with the pancetta and **immediately** stir in the egg mixture while the pasta is still piping hot.
7. Stir to combine, then add just enough of reserved pasta water while continuing to stir to adjust the sauce.
8. Stir in the 2 Tablespoons Pecorino Romano and the parsley.

Season with salt and pepper and serve immediately.

Chef Notes:

- This is a great meal to make for a crowd and it is cheaper then ordering out for pizza. Add garlic bread and a salad and your guests will love it!
- **It is important to have the egg mixture ready when the pasta is done. The hot pasta cooks the eggs.**
- You can substitute Parmesan cheese for Pecorino Romano and bacon for the pancetta

Spaghetti Pie

Ingredients:

- 12 oz. angel hair pasta
- 1 lb. ground beef
- ½ lb. ground Italian sausage
- 1 medium chopped onion
- 2 minced cloves garlic
- 1 large egg
- ¼ cup milk
- 1 teaspoon Italian seasoning
- 24 oz. pasta sauce
- 8 oz. tomato sauce
- ½ cup freshly grated Parmesan cheese and more for topping
- 2 cups shredded mozzarella cheese
- 9-inch refrigerator pie crust

Directions:

1. Preheat the oven to 350° F and lightly spray a 9 x 13-inch casserole dish with cooking spray
2. First, cook the pasta according to the package instructions
3. In a skillet, brown the ground beef and sausage until broken up and cooked through. Drain fat and set meat aside
4. Sauté the onion until translucent, then add the minced garlic and cook for 1 minute
5. Add in the pasta sauce, tomato sauce, and ½ cup Parmesan cheese. Turn off the heat
6. Once the pasta is cooked through, drain it and mix it with the egg, milk, and Italian seasoning.
7. Spread half the pasta in the casserole dish, top with half the meat, and add 1 cup mozzarella cheese. Repeat the layers.
8. Slice the piecrust into 1-inch strips and lay over the cheese horizontally, trimming to fit.
9. Sprinkle Parmesan cheese over the top and bake for 25 minutes.

Entrées: Pork and Ham

Maple-Coated Bacon

Ingredients:

- 1 pound sliced bacon
- ¼ cup pure maple syrup
- 2 Tablespoons wine vinegar
- 1 teaspoon finely grated orange zest
- 1 teaspoon finely grated lime zest
- Freshly snipped chives, for garnish

Directions:

1. Light a grill or preheat a grill pan
2. In a small bowl, whisk the maple syrup with the vinegar and orange and lime zests
3. Grill the bacon over moderately low heat, turning occasionally, until lightly browned and tender, about 12 minutes
4. Brush with the maple-citrus syrup and continue grilling, turning occasionally, until glazed, and cook 2 to 3 minutes longer
5. Transfer the bacon to a platter, garnish with snipped chives, and serve

Sweetened Ham Roast

*This recipe is **so** easy and **so** delicious! A must try for sure. Perfect for holidays, family get togethers, or any night you decide to make something amazing.*

Ingredients:

- 1 pre-cooked ham
- ½ cup strawberry jam
- 2 Tablespoons Dijon mustard
- 1 cup brown sugar
- ½ teaspoon ground cinnamon
- Whole cloves

Directions:

1. Preheat your oven to 400° F.
2. Put your ham in a baking dish. With a sharp knife make diagonal cuts about ¼-inch deep on the top of the ham, making large diamonds on the top.
3. In a small saucepan on medium high put in the strawberry jam. Heat it up for about 1 to 2 minutes, just until you see it melting down a little. Turn off the heat. To that add the brown sugar, Dijon mustard, and cinnamon. Stir it all together to form a delicious glaze paste.
4. With a rubber spatula coat your entire ham. Use all the glaze! Once the glaze is all over the ham it's time to make it pretty!
5. Place one clove in the middle of each diamond.
6. Pop that beautiful baby in the oven. Let cook for about 20 minutes until you see the ham surface caramelize.
7. Take out of the oven and remove the cloves before serving. Collect all that goodness at the bottom of the pan and serve the juices alongside the ham!

Ham Tips

Cooking a ham is remarkably simple. Ideally, the ham will be moist and tender and the glaze complements but doesn't overwhelm the meat.

- In most supermarkets, cured hams come in five forms: boneless, semi-boneless, bone-in, whole, and half.
- Each of these types is available un-sliced or pre-sliced (often labeled "spiral-sliced").
- Bone-in hams that have been spiral-sliced are recommended because they offer the best flavor with the least amount of post cooking and carving.
- As a rule of thumb, you should allow about ½ pound of ham per person.

With all hams, it is important to read the label. Typically, supermarket hams are wet-cured, a process that involves soaking the ham in brine. During this process, the ham will absorb water and gain weight.

- Hams that gained the least water weight (labeled "ham with natural juices") taste the best.
- Avoid labels that read, "ham with water added" or "ham and water products."

Whole ham is the entire leg of the animal. Half hams are available in two distinct cuts: shank end (the bottom part of the leg) and sirloin end (the portion of the leg closer to the rump). It's easy to identify half hams by their shape

- Shank hams have a pointed end much smaller than the larger end. The shank end is easer for carving, since the bone is relatively straight
- The sirloin (or butt) end is rounded. The sirloin end tends to be meatier and less fatty and will not disappoint.

There is nothing you have to do to serve a cured and cooked ham other than cut it off the bone. However, when ham is the centerpiece of a holiday dinner, most people prefer to have it served warm, and often with a glaze. A temperature between 110° F and 120° F is enough to take the chill off the meat without drying it out.

When fully cooking a ham, first, leave the ham at room temperature for 90 minutes prior to cooking. Roasting the ham in an oven bag produces the moistest ham in the least amount of time. If an oven bag is unavailable, aluminum foil will work, but you will have to add three to four minutes of cooking time per pound of meat. Roast the ham in a 250° F oven, which lessens the temperature differential between the exterior and the interior of the roast. Be careful to avoid recipes recommending cooking the ham at 350° F, because by the time the center finally comes up to temperature, the exterior is parched.

A lot of hams come with a packet of premixed glaze. Glaze is a good idea, but the stuff in the packets usually taste awful. Take 10 minutes to make your own glaze.

When we cook ham inside an oven bag, we need a new approach to glazing. Once the internal temperature of the ham reaches 100° F, cut open the bag and increase the oven temperature to 350° F. Apply the glaze and bake the ham for 10 more minutes. Remove the ham from the oven, apply more glaze, and tent the ham with aluminum foil for a 15-minute rest, which allows the internal temperature to increase. Make a side serving sauce with the remaining glaze and the drippings from the oven bag.

Pineapple Glazed Ham

Makes 14 to 18 servings

Ingredients:

- 4 cups pineapple juice
- 1-inch piece fresh ginger, peeled and sliced thinly
- 4 garlic cloves, minced
- 7- to 9-pound bone-in smoked, fully-cooked ham
- 12 to 16 whole cloves
- ¼ cup Dijon mustard
- 1 cup firmly packed light brown sugar
- 20-ounce can pineapple slices in juice, drained
- 10 maraschino cherries, halved

Directions:

1. Stir together first 3 ingredients in a saucepan and bring to a boil. Reduce heat to medium-low and simmer 25 minutes or until liquid is reduced by half. Pour mixture through a wire mesh strainer into a bowl, discarding solids
2. Remove skin and excess fat from ham. Make ¼-inch-deep cuts in a diamond design, and insert cloves at 1-inch intervals. Place ham in an aluminum foil-lined roasting pan
3. Spread Dijon mustard evenly over ham. Pat brown sugar on top of the mustard. Pour pineapple juice mixture into pan
4. Arrange pineapple and cherries evenly over mustard layer on ham and secure with wooden picks
5. Bake at 325° F for 1 hour. Shield with aluminum foil after 1 hour to prevent excess browning, and bake 1 to 1½ hours more or until a meat thermometer inserted into thickest portion registers 140°
6. Baste every 30 minutes with pan juices
7. Remove ham from pan and let stand for 15 minutes before slicing
8. Remove and discard fat from drippings. Bring drippings to a boil in a small saucepan to reduce liquid. Serve as a warm side sauce with the ham

Pork and Sauerkraut

For the Pennsylvania Dutch, Pork and Sauerkraut is the traditional New Year's Day meal. The Pennsylvania Dutch believe eating this on New Years Day brings good luck to the diners in the year ahead. This is usually served with Mashed Potatoes and Baked Beans

Ingredients:

- 1 Boston butt (bone-in pork shoulder roast: 4 to 6 pounds)
- 2 pounds smoked sausage and/or all-beef hot dog combination
- 2 bags (12 to 16 oz. each) fresh sauerkraut
- 2 Tablespoons brown sugar
- 1 favorite variety eating apple

Directions:

1. Add ½ bag of sauerkraut to bottom of a large pot.
2. Arrange pork roast and sausage on top of first layer of sauerkraut
3. Add remaining sauerkraut around and on top of meat
4. Sprinkle with brown sugar and put apple in over the pork roast
5. Cover and cook on low to medium heat until the pork roast is fork tender
6. See **Mashed Potato** and **Baked Beans** recipes for serving sides with the Pork and Sauerkraut

Maple Roasted Pork Terderloin

Ingredients:

- 1 teaspoon whole black peppercorns, plus freshly ground black pepper, for seasoning
- 6 whole garlic cloves, peeled and minced
- 4 allspice berries
- 3 juniper berries
- ⅓ cup kosher salt, plus more for seasoning
- 2 cups apple cider
- ½ cup pure maple syrup
- ⅓ cup brown sugar
- 4 pork tenderloins
- ¼ cup canola oil

Directions:

1. In a medium saucepan toast the black peppercorns with the cloves, allspice, and juniper over moderate heat until fragrant, 2 minutes. Add the salt and the apple cider, syrup, sugar, garlic, and thyme to the saucepan and bring just to a simmer, stirring. Add 3 cups cold water and pour the brine into a small roasting pan; let cool. Add the pork tenderloins, cover, and refrigerate for 6 to 8 hours

2. Preheat the oven to 350°F

3. Drain the pork, discarding the brine. Pat the pork dry and season lightly with salt and pepper

4. In a very large skillet, heat 2 Tablespoons of the canola oil until shimmering. Add 2 of the pork tenderloins and cook over moderately high heat, turning, until browned all over, about 8 minutes. Transfer the pork to a rimmed baking sheet. Wipe out the skillet and repeat with the remaining 2 Tablespoons oil and 2 tenderloins

5. Transfer the pork to the oven and roast for about 18 minutes, turning twice, until an instant-read thermometer inserted in the thickest part of the meat registers 140°F

6. Transfer the pork to a cutting board and let rest for 10 minutes. Slice the pork into medallions and serve

Pulled Pork

Ingredients:

- 1 Boston butt (bone-in pork shoulder roast: 5 to 7 pounds)
- 3 Tablespoons basic barbecue rub
- 1 cup cider vinegar
- 1 Tablespoon coarse salt
- 1 Tablespoon brown sugar
- 1 teaspoon black pepper
- 1 teaspoon pepper flakes
- 12 hamburger buns

Directions:

1. Sprinkle the pork shoulder on all sides with the rub, patting it onto the meat with your fingers. Grill right away or let stand in the refrigerator, covered, for up to 24 hours. The longer you cure it, the richer the flavor will be.

2. Set up the grill for indirect grilling and preheat to medium-low. If using charcoal, place a large drip pan in the center. If using a gas grill, place all the wood chips in the smoker box or in a smoker pouch and preheat to high until you see smoke, then reduce heat to medium-low.

3. Combine the next ingredients for the vinegar basting sauce with ½ cup water in a nonreactive bowl and stir until the salt and brown sugar dissolve. When ready to cook, place the pork, fat-side up, in the center of the hot grate, away from the heat. Cover the grill and cook the pork until very tender, 4 to 6 hours (about 195° F on an instant-read meat thermometer). If using charcoal, add fresh coals and wood chips. Every hour baste the pork with the vinegar sauce.

4. Transfer the cooked pork to a cutting board, cover loosely with aluminum foil, and let rest for 15 minutes. When ready to serve, wearing rubber gloves, pull off the skin and fat. Finely chop the crisp skin with a cleaver to add to the pulled pork or discard. Discard the fat. Pull the pork into shreds about 2 inches long, going along the grain, or chop it with a cleaver.

5. Transfer the shredded pork to a roasting pan and stir in 1 to 1½ cups of the vinegar sauce, enough to keep the pork moist. Cover with aluminum foil and keep warm.

To serve, mound the pork on hamburger buns and top with coleslaw (See **Coleslaw** recipe). Serve any remaining vinegar sauce on the side.

Honolulu-Style Spareribs

These ribs are really tasty and finger-licking yummy!

by Ed Gallagher
Serves 6

Ingredients:

- 4 lbs. meaty pork ribs, cut into 1 or 2 pieces
- 1 lemon, sliced
- 4 sprigs parsley
- 1 sprig fresh oregano or ¼ teaspoon dried oregano
- 2 Tablespoons soy sauce
- 2 Tablespoons dry sherry
- 2 Tablespoons honey
- 1½ teaspoons fresh ginger root, finely chopped
- 1 clove garlic, finely chopped
- ¼ teaspoon five-spice powder*
- ¼ teaspoon pepper
- ¼ cup chili sauce
- ¼ cup peanut oil

Directions:

1. Place ribs in large pot. Add water to cover. Add lemon slices, parsley, and oregano, Bring to a boil. Lower heat and simmer, partially covered, for 45 minutes. Drain. Place in shallow non aluminum dish.

2. Combine soy sauce, sherry, honey, ginger root, garlic, five-spice powder, pepper, chili sauce, and peanut oil in a small bowl. Mix well. Pour mixture over ribs; turn to coat. Cover the ribs and refrigerate for 1 hour.

3. Prepare the grill to medium heat.

4. Brush grill with oil. Grill ribs, covered, over medium heat, basting the ribs often with remaining marinade, until the ribs are crisp about 6 minutes per side.

*NOTE: If you can't find five-spice powder, you can make your own: Combine 1 teaspoon cinnamon, 1 teaspoon crushed anise seed, ¼ teaspoon pepper, and ⅛ teaspoon ground cloves. Store in airtight container. Makes about 2½ teaspoons.

Entrées: Poultry

Jane's Beer Can Chicken

Serves: 4 to 6

Method:

    Indirect grilling and smoking

    1½ cups mesquite chips, soaked in cold water for 1 hour and drained

    Kitchen stores sell a metal stand to hold the beer can and chicken upright for grilling

Ingredients:

    1 large whole chicken (4 to 5 pounds)

    3 Tablespoons of your favorite dry barbecue rub (or see recipe in Notes section)

    12-ounce can beer

Directions:

1. Remove and discard the fat just inside the body cavities of the chicken. Remove the neck and package of giblets. Rinse the chicken, inside and out, under cold running water. then drain and pat dry, inside and out, with paper towels.

2. Sprinkle 1 Tablespoon of the rub inside the body and neck cavities, then rub another 1 Tablespoon all over the skin of the bird. If you wish, rub another ½ Tablespoon of the mixture between the flesh and skin.

3. Set up the grill for indirect grilling, placing a drip pan in the center. If using a charcoal grill, preheat it to medium. If using a gas grill, place all the wood chips in the smoker box and preheat the grill to high; then, when smoke appears, lower the heat to medium.

4. Pop the tab on the beer can. Using a "church key"-style can opener, make 6 or 7 holes in the top of the can. Pour out the top inch of beer, then spoon the remaining dry rub through the holes into the beer. Holding the chicken upright, with the opening of the body cavity down, insert the beer can into the cavity.

5. When ready to cook, if using charcoal, toss half the wood chips on the coals. Oil grill grate. Stand the chicken up in the center of the hot grate, over the drip pan. Spread out the legs to form a sort of tripod, to support the bird.

6. Cover the grill and cook the chicken until fall-off-the-bone tender, 2 hours. If using charcoal, add fresh coals and wood chips after 1 hour.

7. Using tongs, lift the bird to a cutting board or platter, holding a large metal spatula underneath the beer can for support. (Have the board or platter right next to the bird to make the move shorter. Be careful not to spill hot beer on yourself.) Let stand for 5 minutes before carving the meat off the upright carcass. (Toss the beer can out along with the carcass).

Notes:

Ingredients for Basic Rub for Barbecue:

    ½ cup kosher salt

    ½ cup sugar

    ½ cup ground black pepper

    ½ cup paprika

Broccoli and Chicken

This is Rachel & T.J. Rank's go-to dinner

Ingredients:

    1 pound boneless, skinless chicken breast, cut into 1-inch pieces

    2 garlic cloves, finely chopped

    2 teaspoons ginger, finely chopped

    1 cup chicken broth

    3 Tablespoons soy sauce

    2 teaspoons sugar

    2 cups broccoli flowerets

    2 teaspoons cornstarch

Directions:

1. Spray 12-inch nonstick skillet with cooking spray; heat over medium-high heat.
2. Add chicken, garlic, and ginger. Fry 2 to 3 minutes or until chicken is brown.
3. Add ¾ cup of the broth, soy sauce, and sugar. Cover and cook over medium heat 5 minutes, stirring twice.
4. Add broccoli. Cover and cook about 5 minutes, stirring occasionally, until chicken is no longer pink in center and broccoli are crisp-tender.
5. Mix cornstarch with remaining ¼ cup broth; stir into chicken mixture. Cook, stirring frequently, until sauce is thickened.

Lisa's Chicken and Corn Pie

Ingredients:

Pie filling:

- 1 young chicken
- 1 onion chopped
- 1½ cups milk
- 4 cups fresh corn
- ½ cup cream
- 3 eggs
- salt and pepper to taste

Pie crust:

- 1 cup all-purpose flour
- 5 Tablespoons chilled butter, thinly sliced
- ½ teaspoon salt
- 1 egg yolk
- 2 Tablespoons water

Directions:

1. Wash and cut up the chicken
2. Cover chicken with water in stew pot, add chopped onion and cook for about 1½ hours. Season to taste
3. Make crust dough by sifting flour and salt together into a bowl and working butter into it. Beat egg yolk with the water. Add and mix thoroughly. Divide dough in half and chill
4. Take all the chicken meat off the bones and cut into bite sized pieces
5. Cut the corn kernels from the cobs (use fresh, tender corn). Use the back of the knife to scrape the cob of the remaining corn kernel juice
6. Beat the eggs lightly, and mix with the milk and cream
7. Line a deep pie dish with the lower crust. Take ½ of dough and roll out on a floured board to thickness of ⅛ inch. Leave ½ inch of dough to overhang the pie dish
8. Combine chicken, corn, and milk mixture, and season to taste
9. Pour mixture into lower crust, filling the dish to just below the rim of the pie pan
10. Take remainder of dough and roll out on a floured board to thickness of ⅛ inch. Place dough sheet on top of pie, leaving ½ inch of dough to overhang the pie dish. Pinch upper and lower dough sheets together.
11. Gash a large cross in the center of the top crust and brush top crust with melted butter.
12. Bake in pre-heated oven at 375° F for about a half hour.
13. Thicken the balance of the chicken broth with a little flour mixed with cold water for gravy.

Esther Gallagher's Chicken Gismonda

As a newly married couple, Ed and I would enjoy shopping at King of Prussia Mall. Our favorite store was Wanamaker's (an old Philadelphia department store that no longer exists). I found this recipe on one of their shopping bags!! I've served this dish many, many times, and it never fails to impress our guests.

Ingredients:

Chicken:

- 4 chicken breasts, boned and skinned
- salt and pepper
- flour
- 1 cup bread crumbs
- ¾ cup Swiss cheese, shredded
- 2 Tablespoons butter
- 2 Tablespoons oil
- 1 pound sliced mushrooms, sautéed

Anglaise:

- 1 egg
- 2 Tablespoons oil
- ½ cup water
- salt and pepper to taste

Directions:

1. Flatten chicken breasts as much as possible. Sprinkle with salt and pepper
2. Mix bread crumbs and Swiss cheese together and place in flat dish
3. Beat together the Anglaise ingredients in a separate flat dish
4. Coat each flattened chicken breast in flour, then in the Anglaise mixture, and finally in the bread crumb-and-cheese mixture
5. In a large frying pan, melt the butter and oil and saute chicken breasts until completely cooked and golden brown

To serve, top chicken breasts with sauteed mushrooms

Aunt Marta's Chicken Potato Chip Casserole

Yield: 6 servings

Ingredients:
- 4 Tablespoons butter
- 4 Tablespoons flour
- 1 cup chicken broth
- 2½ cups bite-sized chicken pieces
- 2 teaspoons minced onion
- 1 cup diced celery
- ½ cup chopped almonds (optional)
- 2 hard-cooked eggs, diced
- ½ teaspoon salt
- ¼ teaspoon pepper
- ½ Tablespoon Worcestershire sauce
- 1 Tablespoon lemon juice
- ¾ cup mayonnaise
- 1 cup crushed potato chips

Directions:
1. Melt butter; add flour. Stir until smooth and then stir in broth
2. Cook, stirring constantly, until mixed and thickened
3. Add all other ingredients except potato chips
4. Arrange layer of chips in bottom of dish; add chicken mixture
5. Top with remaining chips
6. Bake at 400° F degrees or until bubbly and chips are browned

Chicken Fajitas

This is a Rachel & T.J. Rank's go-to dinner recipe!

Ingredients:

Mix:

- 1 red pepper
- 1 green pepper
- 1 large onion
- fresh salsa
- 1 lb. chicken breasts cut into ½-inch wide strips
- cayenne pepper
- black pepper
- minced garlic clove or garlic powder

Additional:

- fajita wraps
- sour cream
- shredded cheddar cheese
- regular salsa (if you like)

Directions:

1. Cut the red and green peppers into strips and the onion into rings
2. Season the chicken to your liking with the cayenne and black pepper and garlic powder, if no minced garlic is available
3. Sauté the veggies in a large skillet (with the minced garlic if you have it) until tender. Remove the pepper and onion mix from the skillet
4. Cook the chicken in the same skillet until browned
5. Pour the veggies back in with the chicken and mix thoroughly
6. Add 2 cups fresh salsa and mix again. Cook on low heat until the mix is hot

Serve on fajita wraps with sour cream, shredded cheese, and additional salsa

Lebanon's Firehouse Chicken

Ingredients:

Barbecue Sauce:

½ cup oil

¾ cup vinegar

¼ cup water

1½ Tablespoons salt

3 Tablespoon sugar

1½ Tablespoons Worcestershire sauce

1½ Tablespoons Tabasco Sauce (optional if you want a spicy chicken)

Directions:

1. Start a hot charcoal or gas grill
2. You should put an aluminum drip pan over the heat source and under the chicken to manage grease flare-ups. Also, adjust the cooking distance from the coals or heat source
3. Combine all ingredients to make barbeque sauce. Heat if necessary to dissolve salt and sugar
4. Wash and cut whole chicken in half. Cut out the backbone and score the inside center of the breastbone to pull it out and finish splitting the chicken in half
5. Add chicken halves to the grill; brush the barbeque sauce liberally on both sides of the chicken halves
6. Watch the cooking process for grease flare-ups and brush on additional barbecue sauce frequently
7. Cook until chicken falls off the bones or reaches a temperature of 165° F.

See *Jane's Potato Salad* and *Ed's Baked Beans* recipes for great sides

Turkey or Tofu Tacos

Ingredients:

    1 medium carrot, small sweet potato, or small zucchini. I use all 3

    ¼ medium head lettuce

    2 large tomatoes

    7 ounces low-fat cheddar cheese

    15½-oz. can low-sodium pinto beans

    oil or cooking spray

    1 lb. lean ground turkey or tofu

    15½-oz. can chopped or crushed tomatoes, no salt added

    1 Tablespoon chili powder

    1 teaspoon garlic powder

    1 teaspoon dried oregano

    ½ teaspoon salt

    ½ teaspoon ground black pepper

    16 taco shells

Directions:

1. Rinse, peel and grate carrot, sweet potato, or zucchini. Squeeze dry with paper towels
2. Rinse and shred lettuce, Rinse, core, and chop tomatoes
3. Grate cheese
4. In a colander, drain and rinse beans
5. Coat a large skillet with nonstick cooking spray or oil. Heat over medium-high heat. Add turkey or tofu and brown
6. Add grated veggies, beans, canned tomatoes, chili powder, garlic powder, oregano, salt, and black pepper. Stir well
7. Reduce heat to medium. Cook until thickened about 20 minutes.
8. Add 2 Tablespoons cooked meat or tofu mixture to each taco shell. Top each with 1 Tablespoon grated cheese, 1 Tablespoon shredded lettuce, and 1 Tablespoon fresh tomatoes

Chef's Notes:

- I add the cheese right into the skillet. People always wonder why mine tastes better.
- Top tacos with any of your favorite veggies, hot sauce, salsa, low-fat sour cream or low-fat plain ogury
- For more heat, add hot peppers to sauce in step 6.
- You can also use the above ingredients with the addition of black beans and corn to make quesadillas.

Potatoes and Starches

Baked Potatoes

Ingredients:

    Recommend using Russet or Idaho potatoes

    Prepare to offer a serving bar of your favorite potato toppings;

- Butter
- Sour cream
- Crumbled bacon
- Shredded cheese
- Chopped scallions or chives
- Chili sauce with beans and hamburger
- Course salt & ground pepper

Directions:

1. Wash and dry the potatoes
2. Use a fork to puncture holes into the potato on all sides. This helps the steam escape and cook the potato
3. Rub vegetable or olive oil over the potato's skin
4. Sprinkle kosher or a course salt over the potatoes.
5. Place potato directly onto the oven racks so heat can reach all sides of the potato (never wrap potatoes in aluminum foil because this prevents the steam from escaping)
6. Cook For 45 minutes at 450°F, turn heat down to 375°F, and cook 1 to 2 hours (if you are in a hurry, you could initially microwave the potatoes on high for a minute)
7. Total cooking time depends on the size and quantity of potatoes you are baking. Test potatoes with fork to verify completion. Potato skin should break apart easily

Serve with your topping bar of goodies

Esther Gallagher's Hash Brown Potato Casserole

This is a nice change from mashed or scalloped potatoes and it's sooooo easy!

Serves 8 to 10

Ingredients:

- 2 lbs. frozen hash brown potatoes, thawed
- 1 teaspoon salt
- ½ teaspoon pepper
- 10-oz. can cream of chicken soup
- ½ cup chopped onions
- 1 pint sour cream
- 10 oz. shredded cheddar cheese
- ¾ cup melted butter, divided
- 2 cups corn flakes

Directions:

1. Mix together first 7 ingredients with ½ cup of the melted butter
2. Place in a greased 9 x 13 baking dish
3. Crush corn flakes with remaining ¼ cup melted butter
4. Spread corn flake mixture over the top of potato mixture.
5. Bake at 350° F for 1 hour, covered with foil. Remove foil during last 15 minutes

Mashed Potatoes

Ingredients:

   3 pounds potatoes

   2 Tablespoons salt

   1 cup half-and-half, or try a mixture of whole milk and sour cream

   4 Tablespoons sweet butter, melted

   1 teaspoon salt

   ½ teaspoon ground black pepper

Directions:

1. Peel and slice potatoes ½ inch thick
2. Place potatoes in large pot and cover with 1 inch of water. Add 2 Tablespoons salt
3. Cover with lid and place over high heat until boiling
4. Reduce heat and simmer potatoes 15 to 20 minutes, until tender
5. Drain potatoes in a colander
6. Place half-and-half and butter in another pot and warm slowly
7. Add the potatoes back to their cooking pot. Add partial amount of milk-and-butter mixture and begin mashing potatoes with a masher. Add additional liquid mixture until mashed potatoes are smooth, firm, and creamy
8. Add in salt and pepper to taste

Optionally garnish with chopped chives, scallions, or parsley

Jane's Potato Salad

Makes 8 To 10 servings
Preparation Time: 20 minutes
Cooking Time: 40 minutes

Ingredients:

- 4 pounds baking potatoes (8 large), peeled and quartered
- 3 hard-cooked eggs, chopped
- 2 celery ribs, diced,
- ½ small sweet onion, diced
- 1 cup mayonnaise
- 1 Tablespoon yellow mustard
- 1½ teaspoons salt
- ¾ teaspoon pepper

Directions:

1. Cover potatoes in salted water, bring to a boil, and reduce heat to simmer. Cook until potatoes are tender, 40 minutes
2. Drain and cool. Cut potatoes into 1-inch cubes
3. Stir together potato cubes, grated eggs, diced celery, and onions
4. Combine mayonnaise and remaining ingredients for dressing, or use Brenda's Salad Dressing Recipe for a great alternative
5. Gently stir dressing mixture into potato mixture
6. Season with salt and pepper to taste

Serve immediately, or cover and chill.

Variations:

- **Red Potato Salad:** Substitute 4 pounds red potatoes (8 large red potatoes) for baking potatoes
- **Potato Salad With Sweet Pickle:** Add ⅓ cup sweet gherkin pickles cubed, or sweet pickle relish to potato mixture
- **Light Potato Salad:** Substitute 1 cup low-fat mayonnaise or light ranch dressing or greek yogurt

Joyce's Old-Fashioned Warm German Potato Salad

Ingredients:
- 18 small red potatoes, scrubbed
- 4 slices bacon, fried crisp and crumbled
- ½ cup pimento, diced
- 1 sweet onion, diced
- ¼ cup celery, diced
- 2 Tablespoons reserved bacon grease
- ¼ cup wine vinegar
- 1 Tablespoon flour or cornstarch
- ¾ cup chicken broth
- ¼ cup sugar
- ½ teaspoon dry mustard
- 1 teaspoon celery seed
- 2 Tablespoons fresh chopped parsley
- salt and pepper to taste

Directions:
1. Just cover potatoes in salted water, bring to a boil, and reduce heat to simmer. Remove and drain when potatoes are fork tender
2. Mix crumbled bacon, pimento, onion, and celery with potatoes, and season with salt and pepper
3. In skillet, heat bacon grease and stir in vinegar, chicken broth, sugar, and dry mustard and celery seed. Thicken with cornstarch
4. Cut potatoes into cubes and pour liquid over potatoes and let marinate for 3 hours
5. Heat everything over low heat when ready to serve and garnish with parsley

Lisa's Potato Spears (A Baked French Fry)

Ingredients:

4 large potatoes
1 Tablespoon olive oil
Paprika to taste

Directions:

1. Preheat oven to 450° F
2. Scrub potatoes well. Cut lengthwise into six wedges, the size and shape of dill pickle spears. Dry on a paper towel
3. In a large bowl, toss potato spears with olive oil until they are well coated
4. Spread on a baking sheet and dust with paprika
5. Bake 20 to 30 minutes, until tender

Crispy Smashed Potatoes

Serves 8 - 10

Ingredients:

- 24 small white or red skin baby potatoes
- ¼ cup olive oil
- 1 heaping Tablespoon grated Parmesan cheese
- 4 cloves garlic, minced
- ½ teaspoon Italian seasoning
- ½ teaspoon salt
- ¼ teaspoon pepper

Directions:

1. Preheat oven to 450° F
2. Wash potatoes, leaving skins on
3. Place potatoes in a large pot of salted water covered by one inch of water, bring to a boil, and then simmer for about 10 minutes or until they are fork tender
4. While potatoes are boiling, combine the Parmesan cheese and the remaining ingredients in a bowl
5. Spray a large baking sheet with cooking oil. Place drained potatoes about an inch apart on baking sheet. Lightly smash each potato with a fork, breaking them open slightly
6. Cover each potato with a sprinkling of seasoning mixture and olive oil
7. Bake in 450° F oven for 20 minutes or until potatoes are crispy and golden brown

Drunken Coconut Rice

Ingredients:
- 1½ cups rice
- 1 onion chopped
- ½ cup shredded coconut
- 1 Tablespoon curry powder
- 2 Tablespoons butter
- 2½ cups chicken stock or water
- ½ cup Coco Lopez or any cream of coconut
- ½ cup rum
- ½ teaspoon salt

Directions:
1. Sauté onion, coconut, rice, and curry powder until coconut is lightly toasted
2. Add stock, cream of coconut, and salt to the rice mixture
3. Simmer until rice is cooked, 15 to 20 minutes

Chef Notes:
- As long as you have opened a can of Coco Lopez and have the rum out, you might as well make a Piña Colada.

Scalloped Potatoes and Chives

Makes 6 servings

Ingredients:

2½ pounds Yukon Gold potatoes, peeled and thinly sliced

Olive or vegetable oil spray

1 garlic clove, split

1 teaspoon butter

1 medium onion, thinly sliced

½ teaspoon black pepper, plus additional to taste

2 Tablespoons flour

2 cups lowfat milk

1 cup defatted lower-sodium chicken broth

3 Tablespoons snipped chives

Directions:

1. Preheat the oven to 375° F. Lightly coat a 2-quart baking dish with oil spray and rub with the cut sides of the garlic clove

2. Melt the butter in a medium-sized skillet. Add the onion and cook over medium heat, stirring frequently, until it begins to soften, about 4 minutes. Add the salt and pepper and stir to continue

3. Cover the bottom of the baking dish with about one third of the potatoes placed edge to edge. Spread with half the onion mixture and sprinkle with half the flour. Make another layer of potatoes and spread with the remaining onions and flour. Top with a layer of potatoes

4. Heat the milk and broth to simmer in a saucepan and pour over the potatoes. The liquid should come just to the top of the potatoes. Sprinkle with salt and pepper

5. Bake, uncovered, until the potatoes are soft and most of the liquid is absorbed, 50 to 60 minutes

Sprinkle with chives before serving

Note:

- If you can't find Yukon Gold potatoes, you can substitute all-purpose potatoes, decreasing the flour in the recipe to 1 Tablespoon

Wild Rice and Savory Mushrooms

Ashley Edwards

This recipe is a great side dish and goes well with poultry or pork.

Ingredients:
- ½ Tablespoon lemon juice
- 1 Tablespoon soy sauce
- 1 teaspoon sugar
- 2 Tablespoons olive oil
- 1 Tablespoon butter
- 2 teaspoons garlic paste or 2 cloves minced garlic
- 8-oz. package mushrooms
- 1 package long grain and wild rice (I use Uncle Ben's™)

Directions:
1. Quarter the mushrooms and start the rice as package directs
2. Stir together lemon juice, soy sauce, and sugar. Set aside
3. In 12-inch nonstick skillet, heat butter, olive oil, and garlic over medium-high heat until butter melts and garlic becomes aromatic, 3 to 4 minutes
4. Add mushrooms and sauté, stirring until golden brown and butter has been absorbed, 5 - 10 minutes
5. Add lemon mixture to mushrooms, stirring until sauce is absorbed

Spread mushrooms over rice or mix them together — the choice is yours

Chef's Note:
- I almost always double the mushroom part of the recipe. Note: if you just make the mushrooms, they are awesome on top of steak

Macaroni and Cheese

Ingredients:
- 10 Tablespoons unsalted butter
- 1 lb. elbow macaroni
- 4 cups milk
- 6 Tablespoons flour
- 1 teaspoon salt
- cayenne pepper, to taste
- 2 cups shredded sharp Cheddar cheese (half a pound)
- 2 cups shredded Asiago cheese
- 2 cups shredded Fontina cheese
- 1 cup panko bread crumbs
- ½ cup shredded Parmesan cheese

Directions:
1. Preheat the oven to 350° F
2. Butter a 9 x 13-inch baking dish or a 2½-quart casserole
3. Bring 6 quarts of water to a boil, add the pasta and cook, stirring occasionally until *al dente*, approximately 10 minutes
4. Drain the pasta and rinse with cold water, drain again, and place in a large bowl
5. Heat the milk to a boil, then remove from heat (or heat milk in microwave)
6. In a medium, heavy-bottomed saucepan over medium heat, melt 8 Tablespoons butter, reduce heat to low, and whisk in flour. Cook for 3 to 4 minutes, being careful not to brown the mixture. Slowly add the hot milk, whisking constantly to ensure that no lumps will form. Add the salt and cayenne, raise the heat to medium, and simmer until the mixture has thickened, about 8 minutes
7. Remove from heat and add 1 cup each of the shredded Cheddar, Asiago, and Fontina cheeses until they are melted
8. Pour the cheese sauce over the pasta and toss to coat evenly
9. Place half the pasta in the buttered baking dish and distribute the remaining shredded Cheddar, Asiago, and Fontina cheeses over the top. Cover with remaining pasta
10. In a mixing bowl, toss together bread crumbs and parmesan in 2 Tablespoons melted butter. Pour over the pasta and distribute over the top. Bake on the middle shelf of the oven until the top is light brown and mixture is bubbling, 30 to 35 minutes

Vegetables

Mom's 5-Bean Salad

Ingredients:

Beans:

- 1 medium can cut green beans — fresh is better
- 1 medium can cut yellow beans — fresh is better
- 1 medium can kidney beans
- 1 can chick peas (garbanzo beans)
- 1 can lima beans
- ½ sweet pepper, cut into strips
- 1 medium onion, thinly sliced

Dressing:

- 1 cup sugar
- ½ cup apple cider vinegar
- ½ cup olive oil
- 1 teaspoon salt
- Dash pepper

Directions:

1. Drain liquid from the cans of beans and mix in a large bowl with sliced onion and pepper
2. Mix dressing ingredients together and pour over bean mixture
3. Marinate mixture overnight in the refrigerator — 8 hour minimum
4. Taste to adjust seasoning and serve

Note:
- Using fresh beans is best, but you must blanch them before using

Ed's Baked Beans

I have adapted this recipe from one that I received from my good buddy, John Horst. I think my version is a big improvement over his!! This recipe will feed a crowd of 12 - 15 people

Ed Gallagher

Ingredients:

- 5 15.5-oz. cans red kidney beans, drained
- 14 oz. ketchup
- 1 Tablespoon Tabasco sauce
- ½ teaspoon ground allspice
- 1 cup brown sugar
- 8 slices diced bacon, fried and drained
- 2 onions, chopped
- 1 green pepper, chopped
- 3 tomatoes, chopped

Directions:

1. Mix together ketchup, Tabasco sauce, allspice, and brown sugar
2. Mix all ingredients together. Place in a large 4½ to 5-quart casserole which has been sprayed with non-stick cooking spray. Bake at 350° F for about 3 hours

Notes:

- You can use a combination of a variety of beans instead of the red kidney beans, such as pink kidney, white kidney, pinto, or black beans, drained

Brenda's Calico Beans

Ingredients:

- 1 lb. ground beef, browned
- 1 can butter beans or lima beans
- ½ cup chopped onion
- ½ cup chopped bacon
- ½ cup brown sugar
- ½ cup ketchup
- 1 Tablespoon vinegar
- 1 teaspoon mustard
- 15-oz. can kidney beans or Northern beans
- 1 can pork-and-beans
- Worcestershire sauce, to taste – optional

Directions:

1. Brown the ground beef and drain off the excess fat
2. Preheat oven to 350° F
3. Mix all ingredients in a Dutch oven. Include all liquid from pork and beans, but drain off some of the liquid from other beans — mixture should not be too wet
4. Bake at 350° F for 35 minutes

Tammy Bly's Broccoli Casserole

Ingredients:

    2 packages frozen chopped broccoli

    1 can cream of mushroom soup

    1 cup mayonnaise

    2 eggs

    1½ cups grated sharp cheddar cheese

Directions:

1. Preheat oven to 350° F
2. Spray casserole dish sparingly with non-stick cooking spray
3. Prepare frozen broccoli as directed on package
4. Mix remaining ingredients with cooked broccoli and add to the casserole dish.
5. Bake at 350° F for 30 minutes
6. Optional: top with crushed Ritz™ crackers and dot with butter

Note:
- This recipe can be doubled very easily. It may require extra cooking time

Baked Cabbage and Potatoes

This is another John Horst recipe. After all, he is an adopted member of the Clan. This "comfort food" recipe is especially good during the winter because it "sticks to the ribs!"

Ed and Esther Gallagher

Ingredients:

Casserole:

1 lb. cabbage

1 lb. potatoes, peeled and quartered

¼ cup onions, chopped

1 Tablespoon snipped chives

¼ cup butter

Topping:

2 Tablespoons butter

⅔ cup shredded cheddar cheese

1. Remove and discard the core and outer leaves of cabbage. Chop the cabbage.
2. Cook cabbage In boiling salted water for 10 minutes or until tender. Drain the cabbage and refresh it under cold running water. Drain thoroughly.
3. In another pan cook the potatoes In boiling salted water for 20 minutes or until tender. Drain the potatoes and chop them into bite-size pieces. Combine the potatoes with the cabbage.
4. In a skillet, sauté the onions and chives in ¼ cup butter until the onions are softened. Add the mixture to the potatoes and cabbage.
5. Transfer the mixture to a buttered 1½-qt. casserole dish. For the topping, dot it with the butter and sprinkle it with the cheddar cheese.
6. Bake In preheated 350° F oven for 20 minutes or until cheese is melted and vegetables are heated through.
7. Place the casserole under broiler until cheese is lightly browned.

Candied Carrots

Ingredients:

- 1 pound baby carrots or regular carrots cut into 2 inch pieces
- 2 Tablespoons butter, diced
- ¼ cup packed brown sugar
- 1 pinch salt
- 1 pinch ground black pepper

Directions:

1. Place carrots in a pot of salted water. Bring water to a boil, reduce heat to a high simmer, and cook about 20 to 30 minutes. Do not cook the carrots to a mushy stage!
2. Drain the carrots, reduce the heat to its lowest possible setting, and return the carrots to the pan. Stir in butter, brown sugar, salt and pepper. Cook for about 3 to 5 minutes, until sugar is bubbly. Serve hot!

Chinese Veggies and Rice

Ingredients:

    1 cup brown rice

    ½ lb. broccoli

    2 medium celery stalks

    1 medium carrot

    1 small jalapeno or other chili pepper

    1 clove garlic

    6 ounces boneless chicken pieces or firm tofu

    1 Tablespoon cornstarch

    2 teaspoons canola oil

    ½ teaspoon ground ginger (fresh ginger gives more flavor)

Directions

1. Cook rice following package directions. Cover to keep warm
2. Rinse and chop broccoli and celery. Peel and chop carrots,
3. Mince jalapeno. Peel and finely chop garlic
4. If using chicken, remove any skin, then cut chicken into small pieces
5. In a small bowl, stir together soy sauce, brown sugar, and cornstarch. Add 1 teaspoon of the minced jalapeno and stir
6. Heat oil in a medium skillet over medium-high heat. Add ginger and stir. Add chicken or tofu. Cook, stirring occasionally, until slightly browned and starting to cook through, about 2 minutes
7. Add chopped veggies. Stir frequently. Cook until veggies are tender and chicken is completely cooked but not dry, about 5 to 7 minutes
8. Add soy sauce mixture and bring to a boil. Reduce heat and simmer until sauce is slightly thickened, about 2 minutes
9. Serve over warm brown rice

Chef Notes:
- Use only veggies you like. I like to add bok choy. Add veggies with a high water content, like squash or spinach, last.

Mom's Pennsylvania Dutch Chow-Chow

This is a canning pickled vegetable salad recipe to enjoy fresh summer vegetables all winter long. If you don't want to can chow-chow to use in the future, you can also make a smaller batch by just mixing in the pickling liquid and letting it sit at least overnight so the veggies get a "quick pickle."

Makes 2 quarts

Ingredients:

Vegetables:

- 1 cups fresh green beans, cut into bite-size pieces
- ½ pound carrots, peeled and sliced into ½-inch slices
- ¼ whole stalked celery, cut into ½-inch pieces
- ½ sweet onion, chopped
- ½ sweet red pepper, chopped
- ½ head cauliflower, cut into bite-size pieces
- 1 cup small-sized pickling cucumber, cut into about ½-inch slices
- ½ of a 15-oz. can whole kernel corn, drained and rinsed
- ½ of a 15-oz. can kidney beans, drained and rinsed.
- ½ of a 15-oz. can lima beans, drained and rinsed
- Salt to taste

Pickling Liquid:

- 2 cups water
- 2 cups cider vinegar
- 2 cups sugar
- 1 teaspoon salt
- 1 teaspoon celery seed

Directions:

1. Cook the green beans, carrots, celery, onion, pepper, and cauliflower in separate pots until just barely fork tender. Do not cook them all together. Make sure you don't let them get mushy. They should still be slightly crispy. Add some salt to your veggies to taste as they are cooking

2. After all the veggies have cooked, mix together in a large bowl with cucumbers, corn, kidney, and lima beans

3. Fill each canning jar with a mix of the vegetables

4. Mix your pickling liquid ingredients together and heat until the sugar dissolves

5. Pour pickling liquid into each jar. Close jar with a canning lid and ring

6. Proceed to seal jars by putting in a canner. Bring to a boil and cook 10 minutes. After you've removed from the water, you will hear the lids seal.

7. Allow the jars to cool and then store in your pantry. If any of the jars did not seal properly, store in your refrigerator and eat within the next 1 - 2 weeks.

Lisa's Crockpot Cheesy Corn and Peppers

Ingredients:

- 2 pounds frozen corn
- 2 Tablespoons butter, cut into cubes
- 2 Poblano chilis, chopped, or 1 large green pepper and 1 jalapeno, seeded and finely chopped. Personally, I use a small can of green chilis
- 1 teaspoon salt
- ½ teaspoon ground cumin
- ¼ teaspoon ground black pepper
- 1 cup shredded sharp cheddar cheese
- 3 ounces cream cheese, cut into cubes

Directions:

1. Use 3½ to 4-quart crockpot slow cooker with nonstick cooking spray
2. Combine all vegetable ingredients and seasonings in crock-pot. Cook on high 2 hours
3. Stir in cheeses, cover, and cook on high 15 minutes more or until cheese melts

Lisa's Slow-Cooked Corn on the Cob

Ingredients:

6-10 ears of corn husked, with silks removed

Choose the seasoning you would like:

- Olive oil
- Pepper
- Ground cumin
- Curry powder
- Sea salt
- Chili powder
- Fresh lime juice
- Coconut milk

Fresh herbs: dill, thyme, rosemary, sage, tarragon, oregano, or basil

Pesto sriracha sauce

Directions:

Foil Method:

1. Tear/cut pieces of foil big enough to wrap individual ears for corn
2. Put an ear of corn in middle of foil
3. Add seasonings, wrap corn tightly in foil, and place in dry slow-cooker, stem side up, and cover

Approximate cooking times:

- for 4 to 6 ears with the slow cooker approximately ¾ full, cook on high for 2 hours or low for 4 hours
- for 8 to 10 ears with the slow cooker filled all the way to the top, cook on high for 3 hours or low 4 hours

No-Foil Method:

1. Season ears of corn.
2. Brush inside of slow cooker with olive oil or coat with cooking spray, add seasoned corn to slow cooker, and cover

Approximate cooking times:

- for 4 to 6 ears with the slow cooker approximately ¾ full, cook on high for 3 hours or low for 5 hours
- for 8 to 10 ears with the slow cooker filled all the way to the top, cook on high for 4 hours or low for 6 hours

Roasted Corn on the Cob

This makes a fun and great outdoor picnic dish from the grill

Ingredients:

>fresh corn on the cob (1 to 2 ears per person)
>
>butter, melted
>
>salt and pepper to taste

Directions:

1. Pick ears of corn that are fresh, young, and tender and still in the husks. Remove all but the last 3 or 4 husks from each ear of corn
2. Place on the grill for about 4 minutes per side, depending on the heat. Turn several times while grilling to expose all sides of the corn to the heat
3. Corn husks should turn a nice golden, roasted color. The corn silk dries up in this method of cooking and is easy to remove after grilling
4. After cooking, pull back the husks and twist them into a rope to make a nice handle for eating on the cob. Remove any remaining silk
5. Add butter and season with salt and pepper to taste

Corn Pie

Ingredients:

Casserole:

- 1 can corn, drained
- 1 can creamed corn
- 3 potatoes, peeled and cubed
- 4 hard-boiled eggs
- 1 rib celery, diced
- ½ onion, diced
- Milk
- Salt and pepper to taste
- Butter

Biscuit Topping:

- 2 cups Bisquick™
- ⅔ cup milk

Directions:

1. Parboil potatoes
2. Sauté diced celery and onion until translucent
3. Mix potatoes, celery, onions, and corn
4. Pour into sprayed 8 x 8 pan
5. Slice hard-boiled eggs on top
6. Pour milk until almost at top of mixture
7. Add salt and pepper to taste and dot with butter
8. Prepare biscuit topping use dumpling recipe on Bisquick™ box
9. Spoon topping over the corn mixture and bake at 375° F for 40 minutes or until biscuit topping is brown

When serving, put butter pats on top of biscuit topping

Brenda's Baked Lima Beans

Ingredients:

- 1 lb. dried lima beans
- 1 small onion, chopped
- ½ cup catsup
- 1 teaspoon dry mustard
- ⅔ cup brown sugar
- ¼ cup maple syrup
- ¼ lb. sliced bacon

Directions:

1. Soak lima beans in water overnight. Make sure beans are well covered with water as they swell while soaking
2. Drain beans and save the bean water for later use
3. Mix onions with beans
4. Ladle half of beans into a cooking pot. Place strips of bacon over the beans, then ladle the rest of the beans over top of the bacon
5. Combine 2 cups of bean water with catsup, sugar, syrup, and mustard. Stir well and pour over the beans
6. Put the rest of the bacon on top of the beans, then pour the remaining bean water into the pot until the bean mixture is covered
7. Cover pot and bake at 325° F for 3 hours or until the beans are soft. Stir occasionally while baking

Caramelized Onions

Ingredients:

2 Tablespoons extra-virgin olive oil

1 large red, yellow, or white onion (about ¾ pound), peeled, trimmed and cut into ¾-inch pieces

2 Tablespoons balsamic vinegar

Kosher salt

Freshly ground black pepper

Directions:

1. Heat the oil in a 10-inch skillet over medium heat
2. Add the onion and cook, stirring frequently, until lightly browned, about 15 minutes
3. Stir in the vinegar and cook 1 minute longer
4. Season to taste with salt and pepper

Summer Squash Casserole

Esther Gallagher
Serves 8 to 10

Ingredients:

- 6 cups yellow summer squash, sliced
- ¼ cup onions, chopped
- 1 can condensed cream of chicken soup
- 1 cup sour cream
- 1 cup carrots, shredded
- 8-oz. package Pepperidge Farm Herb-seasoned Stuffing Mix™
- ½ cup butter, melted

Directions:

1. Cook sliced squash and onions in boiling salted water for 5 minutes. Drain
2. Combine soup and sour cream. Fold in carrots. Fold in squash and onions
3. Combine stuffing mix with melted butter
4. Spread half of the stuffing mixture in bottom of 13 x 9 inch baking dish. Spoon vegetable mixture on top. Sprinkle remaining stuffing mixture over vegetables
5. Bake in a 350° F oven for 20 to 25 minutes or until bubbly

Notes:
- You could use zucchini or a combination of zucchini and yellow squash in this recipe especially when they are so plentiful in the summer!

Carolina Tomato Pie

Tomato pie is a big item on many menus in the South. We both enjoyed ordering tomato pie while vacationing in Hilton Head, SC. It's a great recipe to use especially when local tomatoes become available up North!

Ed and Esther Gallagher

Ingredients:

- 2 to 3 medium tomatoes, sliced
- ½ cup spring onions, chopped
- ½ cup fresh basil, chopped
- 1 cup (4 oz.) Mozzarella cheese, shredded
- 1 cup (4 oz.) Gruyère cheese, shredded
- ½ cup (2 oz.) Asiago cheese, grated
- ¾ cup mayonnaise
- 9-inch pie crust

Directions:

1. Preheat oven to 350° F
2. Pre-bake the pie shell until almost brown, about 15 to 20 minutes
3. Place tomatoes in colander, sprinkle with salt and pepper, and let drain for about 15 minutes. If tomatoes still appear too wet, place on paper towels and gently blot to dry.
4. In a medium bowl, toss the 3 cheeses with the mayonnaise. Mixture should have the consistency of thick paste
5. Sprinkle chopped onions over bottom of slightly cooled pie crust. Next sprinkle with chopped basil.
6. Layer beginning with sliced tomatoes. Then spread a thin layer of cheese mixture
7. Repeat layers, spreading cheese mixture to edge of pie crust
8. Bake pie at 350° F until top layer bubbles and browns, about 20 minutes
9. Let rest for about 15 minutes

Serve warm.

Thanksgiving Favorites

Brenda's Memories From Earlier Thanksgivings

I have many fond memories of earlier Gallagher Clan Thanksgivings. The holiday would start by going to Aunt Doris Yost's home to watch the Lebanon Thanksgiving Parade. There were no TV's then so we could not watch the Macy's Day Parade.

When I was a bit older, after our Wednesday night supper, we would collect in the kitchen. Grandmother Sadazahn would be there. Someone would get a beer tray and go into the basement to the potato bin and pile the tray high with spuds. Those of us old enough to use a paring knife started peeling. Others would wash and chop celery and onions. There was a parsley patch in the backyard covered with an old rug. One of us was responsible to go down in the dark, cut a bunch of parsley, wash, and snip the leaves with scissors. As the spuds boiled, someone manned the toaster to make the bread cubes. The bread toast was torn into small bits for the filling. The Copes™ Dried Corn was soaking in a bowl of hot water to be cooked in the morning.

Mom would stuff the turkey and it would go into the oven before Mom went to bed, because in the AM the oven was needed for other dishes. Remember Mom's Bread Filling? The Potato Filling would be in a big kettle with its lid on and set outside overnight. Things that were done then would have the culinary police screaming now.

There were only two types of pies; pumpkin and mince. We would have a big bowl of fruit salad; most of it came from cans, but we would add cherries from a jar. Mom would save some juice from the canned fruit and boil it with a box of Jell-O™ added. There was only canned cranberry sauce, but I loved those ridges as the red blob slid out of the can.

Aunt Doris would bring the sweet potatoes loaded with marshmallows. Aunt Jane always had a special apricot Jell-O™. If Pop was lucky on the punchboard, there would be a box of Whitman™ Chocolates.

The 10 Gallaghers, and the Yost and Bleistine families would gather to celebrate Thanksgiving. When it was time to eat, you were lucky to be seated at real and card tables or you just had to balance your full plate on your lap. After dinner, everyone pitched in when it was time to do the dishes. Yes, this was before Lori's and Lisa's time.

Today there are many new traditions along with the old ones. But most importantly, the family LOVE is stronger then ever. I hope as you gather each year, you remember the good times, the love we all received, and the fun we had. I am missing all of you but I will be there in spirit.

HAPPY THANKSGIVING!
Brenda

Brining Your Meats

Brining is the technique of accentuating the taste, texture, and moisture level of leaner cuts of meat (such as turkey, chicken, and pork) through prolonged immersion in salted liquid. It doesn't take much effort, and you've probably already got everything you need on hand.

For the most basic brining, you'll need:

- A plastic, glass, ceramic, or stainless steel (no aluminum) vessel large enough to hold your meat and cover with brine solution
- Salt (either table or kosher)
- Sugar
- Water

To figure out how much brine you'll need, place the meat in the container, and pour in plain water to cover the meat. Measure the water. For every quart, you'll need to add ¼ cup kosher salt (or ⅛ cup table salt) and 2 Tablespoons sugar.

Pour the brine over the meat, place a heavy plate or bowl atop the meat to keep it submerged, and place in the refrigerator or a cooler below 40° F. Different types and sizes of meat will take more or less time. Start at the lower end of the scale and turn the meat halfway through. You can always brine more, but you can't unbrine.

- Chicken (whole): 3 - 8 hours
- Chicken Pieces: 1 - 2 hours
- Game Hens: 1 - 2 hours
- Pork Chops: 2 - 6 hours
- Pork Tenderloin: 2 - 8 hours
- Whole Turkey: 6 - 24 hours

Some recipes call for rinsing the meat afterward and some don't. Either way, make sure to pat it dry before cooking so you're not just steaming the meat.

You can start experimenting with the brine solution by adding sweeteners (like molasses, honey, and syrup), fruit juices, spices, herbs, liquor, peppers, garlic, onions, etc. — wherever your culinary creativity takes you.

Corn Casserole

Makes 7 ½-cup servings
Preparation time: 10 minutes
Total time: 1 hour

Ingredients:

- Nonstick cooking spray
- 2 Tablespoons butter
- ½ cup diced sweet onion
- ¼ cup diced red bell pepper
- ¼ cup diced green bell pepper
- 2 Tablespoons flour
- ¼ teaspoon salt
- ¼ teaspoon ground mustard
- ⅛ teaspoon ground black pepper
- ¾ cup skim milk
- 16-ounce package frozen corn, thawed
- 1 egg, slightly beaten
- ¾ cup Panko bread crumbs or slightly-crushed corn flakes

Directions:

1. Preheat oven to 350° F
2. Coat a 1-quart casserole dish with nonstick cooking spray
3. In a nonstick skillet over medium heat, melt 1 Tablespoon butter
4. Add the diced onion, red pepper, and green pepper to the skillet and cook until crisp-tender, about 3 to 5 minutes
5. Stir in flour, salt, ground mustard, and black pepper. Cook an additional minute, stirring constantly
6. Stir in milk, bring to a boil while stirring constantly, and remove from heat
7. Stir in the corn kernels and egg. Pour into prepared casserole dish
8. In a small bowl, mix breadcrumbs and 1 Tablespoon melted butter into a crumble; then sprinkle crumble over corn mixture
9. Bake uncovered 40 to 45 minutes or until center is set

Cranberry Relish

Ingredients:

- ¼ cup orange juice
- ¼ cup 100% cranberry juice
- 1 cup honey
- 1 pound fresh cranberries

Directions:

1. Rinse and trim cranberries
2. Bring juices and honey to a boil and simmer for 5 minutes
3. Add cranberries and stir for not more then 15 minutes
4. Cranberries should burst
5. Cool and serve

Chuck and Wes' Deep-Fried Turkey

Deep-frying turkeys is a good way to stay out of the hustle in the kitchen and enjoy the outdoors with a beverage or two. It also frees up the oven for cooking all the other delicious Thanksgiving dishes.

Ingredients:

2 12 - 15-lb. turkeys, prefer fresh rather than frozen

Favorite marinade injection sauce

5 gallons peanut oil

Salt and other preferred seasoning ingredients

Safety Precautions:

- The turkeys must be thawed and patted dry before immersing into hot cooking oils. Otherwise, hot cooking oils will erupt and risk oil fires and personal burns causing serious injury.

- Do not overfill the fryer pot with oil. To estimate how much oil you will need, place the Turkey in the fryer pot and fill with cold water until the turkey is submerged. Remove the turkey and note the water level. This is the level of cold oil to add to your fryer.

- Find a level dirt or grassy area outside to position the fryer. Never fry your turkey indoors, in a garage or attached structure, or on a deck.

- Set up a work table in your fryer area. Have a cooking timer, paper towels, serving platters, long oven gloves, and a fire extinguisher on hand. Folding chairs are a good idea too.

- Keep children and pets away from the fryer area. Never leave the hot oil unattended.

- Allow the oil to cool completely after use. Return used oil to original container and recycle.

continued on next page

continued from previous page

Directions:

1. Prep the turkeys the night before frying. Record the turkey weight to calculate the deep-frying time. Remove the giblets, neck, and wing tips and save for gravy stock cooking.

2. Remove all plastic and metal thermometer inserts and leg clips from the turkey. I also remove excess fat globules from the bird. The bird cavity must remain empty.

3. Rinse and drain the turkey. Consider using a Cajun injector to add a marinade to the turkey. Cajun butter is a Gallagher Clan favorite. I always try a different marinade in the second bird. Rub salt and other selected seasonings inside and outside the bird. Refrigerate overnight.

4. Plan your fryer setup for 3 hours before the targeted dinner serving time.

5. Bring your birds to room temperature and pat dry of any residual marinade and moisture both inside and outside the bird

6. Set up your deep fryer station. Add the peanut oil to the determined immersion level in the deep fryer pot. Start up your burner and bring the oil up to 350° F. Have a deep-frying thermometer to continuously monitor the temperature of the oil.

7. Load the turkey onto the frying stand with the legs down and the neck cavity opening up.

8. Calculate the frying time by multiplying the bird weight by 3.5 minutes. For example, a 12-lb. turkey should be deep fried for 42 minutes.

9. Using heat safety gloves and the fryer loading hook, slowly lower the turkey and frying stand into the 350° F cooking oil. Watch out for hot oil splatter. Set your cooking timer.

10. Adjust burner flame to maintain a lower cooking temperature of 325° F for the total frying time. Continuously monitor the oil cooking temperature and adjust burner appropriately. You will need less burner heat to hold the oil at 325° F as the cooking time progresses.

11. After the cooking time has elapsed, remove the turkey slowly to allow the hot oils to drain back into the frying pot.

12. Transfer the fried bird to a serving platter and tent with aluminum foil to let the bird rest.

13. Repeat this process for the second turkey.

14. Carve the turkeys 30 minutes before serving and be sure to save the fried skin!

Pennsylvania Dried Corn

Serves 8 - 10

Ingredients:

    1 box Copes™ dried corn

    1 stick butter

    ¼ cup brown sugar

    Whole milk

    Salt and pepper to taste

Directions:

1. In a crock pot on medium heat, add dried corn, a stick of butter, and whole milk to cover. Stir to melt butter and add brown sugar, stirring until dissolved
2. Stir every 45 minutes and add additional milk to keep corn covered
3. Slow cook for approximately 3 hours
4. Adjust addition of butter, sugar, salt, and pepper to taste

Remove corn to a serving dish

Westley Green Bean Casserole

Ingredients:

- 2 pounds fresh green beans — snap off ends and remove stem strings
- 1 can cream of mushroom soup
- 2 cans sliced water chestnuts, drained and rinsed
- 2 sweet onions, cut into small dice pieces
- 1 lb. grated Cheddar cheese
- 1 can fried onion crisps
- Salt and pepper to taste

Optional ingredients:

- Sliced fresh mushrooms, crumbled bacon, or diced ham can be added depending on personal preferences

Directions:

1. Bring two gallons of salted water to a boil
2. Add half the green beans for a two-minute boil, remove, and place into an ice-water bath
3. Repeat with second half of the green beans
4. Remove beans from the ice bath and pat dry
5. Spray a large casserole dish with nonstick cooking spray
6. Make approximately 3 layers of green beans, water chestnuts, diced onions, grated cheese, and any other optional ingredients. Save extra cheese for the very top layer
7. Mix can of mushroom soup with two cans of whole milk and pour evenly over top of the casserole
8. Bake casserole in 350°F oven for 45 minutes
9. Add onion crisps to the top of the casserole during the last 5 minutes in the oven

Jane Bleistine's Apricot Jell-O™

Ingredients:

- 2 small boxes apricot Jell-O™
- 1 large can crushed pineapple
- about ½ to ¾ bag miniature marshmallows
- 2 to 3 bananas, thinly cut into rounds
- 1 package Philadelphia™ cream cheese (let's not use anything but "Philly," please)
- 1 egg
- 1 regular-size tub cool whip
- 1 teaspoon vanilla (you can use more if you like)
- about 1 Tablespoon flour

Directions:

Jell-O™:

1. Open the can of crushed pineapple and separate the pineapple from the juice
2. Substituting the pineapple juice for water, mix the Jell-O™ as designated on the box in a 13-inch pan
3. After you make the Jell-O™ mixture, add the crushed pineapple. Then add the sliced bananas so that they fully cover the crushed pineapple layer. Top the bananas with miniature marshmallows
4. Place in refrigerator to set for at least 4 hours

Topping:

Okay, here is the hard part. Before you make this, say a prayer and ask Aunt Jane B. to assist you!

1. In a medium-sized pot on low heat slowly melt the Philladelphia™ cream cheese and remove from heat
2. Beat the egg in a bowl and add the vanilla. Slowly add the egg mixture into the melted cream cheese while beating the heck out of the mixture so it doesn't become scrambled eggs
3. Start adding the cool whip. When it gets a little thin, slowly add flour and keep beating the heck out of the mixture until it is a pudding.
4. Pour mixture over hardened Jell-O™. Place in refrigerator and serve after cooled Follow Aunt Jane's tradition of asking everyone if they like her Jell-O™!

Oyster Stuffing

Ingredients:

- 1 package bread stuffing cubes
- 1 cup butter
- 2 cups chopped onions
- 1 Tablespoon minced garlic
- 4 oz. mushrooms, sliced
- 3 dozen shucked oysters with the juice reserved
- 1 lb. Italian sweet sausage, with outer casings removed
- ¼ cup prunes or dates, seeded
- 4 oz. dried cherries
- 4 oz. golden raisins
- 1 teaspoon salt
- ½ cup cream
- ½ cup milk
- 2 Tablespoons minced parsley
- 1 Tablespoon minced sage
- 1 teaspoon minced rosemary
- 1 Tablespoon minced thyme

Directions:

1. Preheat oven to 350° F
2. Melt 1 Tablespoon butter and coat a 2-quart casserole dish
3. Melt 1 Tablespoon butter and add sausage. Break up sausage into small pieces while cooking. Drain fat and set sausage aside
4. Melt 8 oz. butter in a skillet and add onion and garlic. Sauté until translucent
5. Add the mushrooms and continue to sauté for another 3 minutes
6. Add the oysters, oyster juice, cooked sausage, dried fruits, salt, and pepper. Cook for 3 minutes and stir until the mixture is well blended. Remove from heat and set aside
7. In a large bowl, lightly beat the eggs. Add the cream and milk. Stir until this is well blended. Add the parsley, sage, rosemary, and thyme.
8. Add the oyster mixture and bread cubes to the large bowl and mix well. Taste and adjust seasoning with salt & pepper.
9. Transfer to the coated casserole dish and bake for 45 minutes or until done

Uncle Eddie's Pennsylvania Dutch Potato Filling

Serves 35 - 40

Ingredients:

    10 lbs. potatoes, peeled and quartered

    2 cups onions, chopped

    2 cups celery, chopped

    1 large bunch parsley, chopped

    3 8 - 10-oz, packages Kellogg's™ Stuffing Mix or any other stuffing mix/ croutons like Pepperidge Farm™ or Arnold's™

    4 sticks butter

    8 eggs, slightly beaten

    milk or chicken broth, as needed

    salt and pepper to taste

Directions:

1. Cook the potatoes in salted water until tender. Drain and mash the potatoes using a potato masher. Add two sticks of butter along with the beaten eggs. Add enough milk to the mixture until well blended

2. While potatoes are cooking, melt 2 sticks of butter in a pan and sauté the onions and celery, but do not brown. When vegetables are soft, add to the potato mixture along with the chopped parsley. Blend together

3. Place crouton/stuffing mix in the same pan used to cook onions and celery. Pour milk or chicken broth over the stuffing mixture. Use enough liquid to soften the croutons — you do not want them to get mushy. Add the croutons to the potato mixture and blend thoroughly. Season with salt and pepper to taste

4. Place in a large pan and dot with additional butter. Bake in a preheated 350° F oven for about 1½ hours

    ENJOY!!!

Ed Gallagher's Sausage Cranberry Apple Stuffing

I found this recipe in a magazine many years ago. It was a $12,000 grand prize winner. Everyone in the family knows this has become a Gallagher family favorite! It seems Thanksgiving is not complete without Uncle Eddie's sausage stuffing. This makes me very happy knowing I have outdone and outsmarted all of my sisters and brothers, too! **Eddie Rules!**

Ingredients:

- 2 6-oz. boxes Kelloggs Croutettes Stuffing Mix™
- 2 eggs, slightly beaten
- 1½ cups onions, finely chopped
- 2½ cups celery, finely chopped
- ½ cup butter, melted
- 1 pound bulk sausage
- 8-oz. can jellied cranberry sauce, beaten until thin
- 1 to 2 cups apple juice

Directions:

1. Cook sausage until light brown. Drain and place in a small bowl. Sauté onions and celery in butter until tender. Add this mixture to the sausage
2. Next, add stuffing mix, eggs, and cranberry sauce. Mix thoroughly. Add apple juice, a little at a time, until entire mixture is dampened but not mushy
3. Stuff an 18 to 20 pound turkey, or bake in a covered casserole for 30 to 40 minutes in a 350°F oven

Notes:

- Half of this recipe will stuff a 7 to 10 pound turkey
- Sometimes it is difficult to find the Kelloggs Croutettes™ so you might have to substitute Arnold's™ or Pepperidge Farm™ stuffing

Turkey Gravy

For starters, be sure to have plenty of stock on hand so that you will be able to make enough gravy. Use homemade turkey stock (made from the neck and giblets), or canned chicken stock.

makes 2 cups of gravy
(increase ingredients proportionately to make more gravy)

Ingredients:

    2 cups homemade turkey stock or chicken stock

    2 Tablespoons turkey fat

    2 Tablespoons flour

    reserved pan juices

Directions:

1. Pour all the liquid from the roasting pan into a glass measuring cup. Using a spoon, skim as much fat as you can from the surface and set aside. Reserve the remaining dark, rich pan juices
2. Set the roasting pan over two burners on moderate heat. Add turkey fat and whisk in flour, whisking up any browned turkey bits that are stuck to the pan
3. Slowly start adding the stock, whisking constantly to make a smooth paste; then whisk in the rest of the stock
4. Lower the heat to simmer the gravy, whisking occasionally, until the floury taste is gone and the gravy is smooth and thick, at least five minutes
5. Now stir in the reserved pan juices. Season with salt and pepper
6. Pour the gravy through a coarse strainer into a warmed gravy boat
7. Optionally, add cut-up turkey giblets and small trimmings of turkey meat to the gravy

5. Never dip your measuring cup into the flour.

   Dipping a measuring cup into a bag of flour packs the flour into the well of the measuring cup. It may seem like the easiest way to scoop flour, but you're actually getting more flour than you really need. Too much flour will turn into dense breads, hard cookies, and stiff cakes. You need the same amount of flour each time to get consistent results. Try:
   - The less accurate option is to use a spoon to lightly scoop flour into a dry measuring cup, then use a flat edge to level off the flour.
   - The most accurate way to measure flour is with a digital scale. A cup of all-purpose flour should weigh 130 grams.

6. You must preheat your oven.

   Quick and sudden heat is an important part of the baking process. We've all tried to save time and just turn the oven on and stick the pan in. This is a bad idea for the finished quality of your baked good. Try:
   - Letting the dough or batter sit while the oven heats up. Most ovens can be heated in about 10 minutes.
   - If you're working with temperature-sensitive dough, pop the dough into the fridge until the oven is ready.

7. You must confirm your oven's temperature.

   Just because your oven says 350° F doesn't mean it really is. That means your pastries may not bake properly because your oven could be too hot, or even too cool. A temperature difference can have a big effect on the final baked product.

   Invest in an oven thermometer and hang it from your oven rack. Pre-heat your oven fully and see what the thermometer says. This will demonstrate how much you should adjust your oven temperature setting for your proper baking temperature.

8. Never substitute baking powder for baking soda (or vice versa).

   They share a similar name, and even look similar out of the box, but they are quite different. Baking soda must have an accompanying acid (lemon juice, vinegar, buttermilk) to activate it. Baking powder, on the other hand, already contains that acid.

   If you use the wrong one, your baked goods will take a hit.

   Keep both on hand and be sure to check their expiration dates. Expired baking soda and baking powder lose their leavening ability as they age. Expired product may cause your cookies to not spread far enough, or your cakes to not rise properly.

9. Never ignore the "sifted" requirement.

    The recipe is asking you to sift ingredients for a very particular reason, typically that the final baked good's texture is meant to be very light and fluffy. Sifted flour can rise more easily than unsifted flour. Cocoa powder and powdered sugar are also often sifted.

    Invest in buying and using a sifter. As a backup you can gently tap and shake your flour through a fine mesh sieve or colander. Another possibility is using a whisk to help remove lumps and lighten up the ingredients for better mixing.

10. Let butter and eggs warm to room temperature.

    Recipes that require softened butter and cream cheese or room temperature eggs do so for a reason. These ingredients perform differently when they are warmed than when added cold from the fridge. Butter creams more easily and eggs whip faster when at room temperature.

    Take the ingredients you need to warm to room temperature out of the fridge at least 30 minutes before you plan to cook. For large sticks of butter or cream cheese you may need more time. Don't put them near anything hot or they'll be too soft.

11. Avoid over-softening butter in the microwave.

    So you didn't follow the 30-minute warming suggestion and you absolutely cannot wait. You can briefly microwave the butter on low power for 10 to 15 seconds maximum. If it isn't softened, repeat for another 10 to 15 seconds. Just be careful to microwave slowly so you don't end up with a puddle.

12. Never over mix the batter.

    Recipes are written for brevity, so instructions such as "just until mixed" leave a lot of room for interpretation. Unfortunately, over-mixing turns dough and batters into stringy messes, which results in dense and chewy baked goods.

    Try gently mixing any dough or batter until it is uniform with the wet and dry ingredients fully integrated; then just stop mixing. You will get the best final baked textures if you only mix the batter to that fully integrated point.

13. Always cream the butter and sugar a little longer.

    Generally speaking, over-mixing is a bad idea; but when it comes to creaming butter and sugar, you should let the mixer go a bit longer. Combining the two until they are airy and fluffy and you notice a lighter color change will help the batter rise when it's in the oven. Don't rush this step; if you don't cream the butter and sugar until fluffy, your baked goods may be dense.

14. Never risk doubling a recipe to make extra batter.

    Baking doesn't necessarily work when you are just doubling all the ingredients in their proper ratios. While some baked goods recipes can be doubled, don't risk it. It is safer to make two batches of the same recipe rather than one big batch.

15. Practice patience in checking on your baked goods.

    Don't let the excitement of watching your cake rise cause your cake to fall. Every time you open the oven door, you release a lot of heat. Constant interruptions will affect your baking product's outcome. Let the oven work its magic. Use the light inside the oven to watch your baked good rise and gauge how close it is to done. Also, don't remove the pan from the oven to test for doneness. Leave it in, and quickly insert a thermometer or a toothpick to check.

16. Never reuse a hot baking sheet.

    Most cookie recipes make more dough than will fit on a single baking tray. You will need to cook in batches to use all the dough. Never put cold dough on a hot tray.

    The dough will spread too quickly and be browner than it should be.

    Invest in a spare cookie sheet. Alternate cookie sheets with each oven batch. Take the cookie sheet away from the hot stove so that it has a chance to cool. You can put the warm cookie sheet in the freezer for a couple of minutes to speed up the cooling process.

17. Avoid using a dark baking pan without adjusting your oven's temperature.

    Light-colored metal pans are preferred for baking. Most baking recipes assume you will be using a light-colored metal pan. Dark metal pans absorb more heat from the oven than light metal pans.

    If you must use a dark-colored baking pan, consider lowering the oven temperature by 25° F. Your baked product may need a couple of minutes longer to bake, but beyond that, you will risk browning the bottom of your pastry.

18. Let your pastry cool before trying to frost.

    Everyone is anxious to taste your delicious pastry, but you will risk ruining your masterpiece if you frost it before your pastry has a chance to cool. The frosting will melt when added to warm baked goods. Have patience and let your baked goods cool completely to the touch before frosting. If you are in a hurry, you can put your pastry in the refrigerator for a few minutes.

Baking Flavor Enhancement Tips

It is about FLAVOR. The magic of a great baked good or dessert is about the flavor. Enhancers are basic flavors that make other flavors taste more like themselves. So here are the go-to items and how to best employ them!

Instant *Espresso* Powder (Not to be confused with *espresso*-grind coffee)

Adding from a pinch to a teaspoon of this stuff to any chocolate dessert ramps up the chocolate and doesn't add coffee flavor, just a more complex chocolate experience. Mix it in with your dry ingredients and taste the difference.

Lemon

A hint of lemon can intensify the fruitiness of any fruit flavor. The tartness also balances the sweetness that is inherent in fruit and gives a rounder flavor. A little goes a long way here, so start with a little bit and add more if you need it. There are three ways to incorporate lemon into a dish.

- Zest, which gives pure lemon intensity but no liquid. This is great for things like pie filling, where you are trying to limit the excess liquid, or baked goods, where the texture of the zest won't be noticed, like cookies.
- Lemon juice, which is less intense than zest, but more sour, is great for things like jams, where you are using a lot of sugar.
- Lemon paste, which is slightly sweeter and a great addition to batters for cakes or cupcakes, frostings, or fillings.

Nutmeg

Nothing makes vanilla taste more like vanilla than a teensy bit of fresh nutmeg. "Fresh" means a whole nutmeg given a swipe or two across a grater. Pre-ground nutmeg can be a little musty. Creamy desserts are helped with three or four scrapes to rice pudding, bread pudding, pudding, and *crème bruleé*. This subtle spice is often used to enhance cream-based savory sauces like *béchamel,* and to add something special in creamed spinach and mac-and-cheese.

Cinnamon

Cinnamon does for caramel desserts what nutmeg does for vanilla and *espresso* powder does for chocolate. It makes caramel taste even more caramel. Judiciousness is the key: start with little teeny pinches. You can always add more.

Almond extract

Almond is to coffee as coffee is to chocolate. Ask anyone who has ever eaten Jamoca Almond Fudge™ ice cream about the great combination. Whether it is a coffee frosting, coffee ice cream, or a coffee flavored cookie, even a quarter to half teaspoon of almond extract will give it a little sparkle.

White pepper

White pepper is an ingenious ingredient in anything that is flavored with ginger or spice or molasses or all three. If you are making gingerbread cake or molasses cookies, a few fine fresh grinds of white pepper will add a depth to the spiciness with some background floral notes that are just extra.

Salt

Salt is the most important secret weapon. You should use it in every dessert no matter what the flavor profile. Salt balances sweet and enhances all the flavors, whether it is a sprinkle of flaky salt on top of a cookie, or just adding that pinch of kosher salt to a batter or frosting or custard to make sure that balance is in play. Unless a dessert recipe says "don't use salt and this is why," just add it in there.

Amish Shoofly Pie

Ingredients:

1 cup flour

⅔ cup brown sugar

1 rounded Tablespoon shortening or margarine

1 cup molasses

¾ cup hot water

1 egg

1 teaspoon baking soda dissolved in ¼ cup hot water

Pastry for one lower 9-inch crust pie

Directions:

1. Prepare pie pan with lower pie crust
2. Combine flour, brown sugar, and shortening; make crumbs either by hand or using a pastry blender. Set aside ½ cup of crumbs to sprinkle on top of pre-baked pie
3. Combine molasses, hot water, egg, and baking soda dissolved in water; mix well.
4. Stir crumbs into liquid. Pour resulting mixture into pie crust and top with reserved crumbs
5. Bake at 375° F for 35 minutes

Serve — some like whipped cream with their pie

French Apple Crisp

Ingredients:

Filling:

- 3 cups sliced, peeled apples (3 large apples)
- 1 teaspoon ground cinnamon
- ¼ teaspoon ground nutmeg
- ½ cup Original Bisquick™ mix
- ½ cup granulated sugar
- ½ cup milk
- 1 Tablespoon butter or margarine, softened
- 2 eggs

Streusel:

- ½ cup Original Bisquick™ mix
- ¼ cup chopped nuts
- ¼ cup packed brown sugar
- 2 Tablespoons firm butter or margarine

Directions:

1. Heat oven to 325° F. Grease 9-inch glass pie plate
2. In medium bowl, mix apples, cinnamon. and nutmeg; place in pie plate
3. In medium bowl, stir remaining filling ingredients until well blended. Pour over apple mixture in pie plate
4. In small bowl, mix all streusel ingredients until crumbly and sprinkle over filling
5. Bake 40 to 45 minutes or until knife inserted in center comes out clean
6. Cool 5 minutes. Store in refrigerator

Chef Notes:

- Some favorite varieties of apples for baked pies are Empire, Regent, and Spartan
- Substitute 3 cups sliced, peeled pears for the apples to make a French Pear Crisp

Brenda's Glazed Apple Dumplings

Ingredients:

Dumplings:

8 baking apples (e.g., Granny Smith)

Pie dough for a 2-crust pie

Glaze:

1½ cups sugar

6 Tablespoons butter

1½ cups water

1 teaspoon cinnamon

Directions:
1. Preheat oven to 350° F
2. Peel and core apples, but keep them whole
3. Divide dough in 2 equal halves. Roll each half into a circle
4. Cut each circle into 4 pieces
5. Place 1 apple in the center of each triangle and fold dough around apple
6. Place in oblong baking pan
7. Mix glaze ingredients together and bring to a boil
8. Pour glaze over dumplings
9. Bake at 350° F for 35 to 40 minutes, basting every 10 minutes with liquid in pan

Chef Note:
- Baking time varies depending on apple size and firmness: do **not** leave in oven for too long. When apples feel soft, by poking with a knife, remove from oven

Tammy Bly's Blueberry Crumble

Ingredients:

    20-oz. can crushed pineapple

    3 cups fresh or frozen blueberries, sprinkle with ½ cup sugar

    1 box yellow cake mix (dry)

    1 stick melted butter - dribble all over

    1 cup chopped pecans (optional)

    ¼ cup sugar

Directions:

1. Preheat oven to 350° F
2. Spray or butter a 13 x 9 pan
3. Add first 5 ingredients in order listed to cooking pan - **do not stir**
4. Sprinkle top with ¼ cup sugar
5. Bake until bubbly all over, about 45 to 60 minutes

Serve with vanilla ice cream

Chef Note:

- I have recently started using less sugar and it still tastes great

Jane's Krispy Kreme™ Bread Pudding

Ingredients:

- 2 dozen Krispy Kreme™ donuts
- 14-ounce can sweetened condensed (**not** evaporated) milk
- 2 4.5-ounce cans fruit cocktail, undrained
- 2 eggs, beaten
- 9-ounce box raisins
- 1 pinch salt
- 2 teaspoons ground cinnamon
- Butter Rum Sauce (see recipe below)

Directions:

1. Preheat oven to 350° F
2. Cube donuts into bite sized pieces and place into a large casserole bowl
3. Mix other ingredients together and pour on top of donuts
4. Let everything soak for a few minutes, then stir together until donuts have soaked up as much of the liquid as possible
5. Bake for about 1 hour or until center has jelled
6. Top each serving with Butter Rum Sauce

Butter Rum Sauce

Ingredients:

- 1 stick butter
- 1 pound box confectioners' sugar
- Rum, to taste

Directions:

1. Melt butter and slowly stir in confectioners' sugar. Add rum and heat until bubbly.

Pour over each serving of Krispy Kreme™ Bread Pudding

Joyce's Bread Pudding

Ingredients:

> non-stick cooking spray
>
> 1 loaf white bread, or any kind you want
>
> 1 quart milk
>
> 6 beaten eggs
>
> ½ to 1 cup sugar
>
> 1 teaspoon vanilla
>
> Optional: fruit (1 can crushed pineapple, drained, or ½ cup raisins + ground cinnamon to taste)

Directions:

1. Preheat oven to 350° F
2. Remove crusts from bread and rip slices of bread apart into bite-size pieces. Raisin bread is convenient as you can leave out the fruit below
3. Place bread in 13 x 9 pan coated with non-stick cooking spray
4. In a separate bowl, make custard by mixing together the remaining ingredients
5. Push bread down with back of spoon while pouring custard over the bread so that bread is totally submerged, but not floating
6. Bake in preheated 350° F oven until test knife comes out clean

Cream Cheese Flan

Ingredients:

- 1½ cups sugar, divided
- 7 egg yolks
- 14-ounce can sweetened condensed milk
- 12-ounce can evaporated milk
- ¾ cup milk
- 1½ teaspoons vanilla extract
- ⅛ teaspoon salt
- 4 egg whites
- 8-ounce package cream cheese

Directions:

1. Sprinkle 1 cup sugar in a medium-size heavy saucepan; place over medium heat and cook, stirring constantly, 5 minutes, or until sugar melts and turns a light golden brown
2. Quickly pour hot caramelized sugar into a 2-quart flan dish. Using oven mitts, tilt dish to evenly coat bottom and sides. Let stand 5 minutes (sugar will harden).
3. Whisk together egg yolks and next 5 ingredients in a large bowl
4. Process egg whites, cream cheese, and remaining ½ cup sugar in blender until smooth. Stir egg white mixture into egg yolk mixture.
5. Pour mixture through a wire-mesh strainer into a large bowl; pour custard over caramelized sugar.
6. Place dish in a large shallow pan. Add hot water to pan to a depth of one-third up sides of dish. Bake at 350° F for 1 hour and 45 minutes
7. Remove dish from water bath; cool completely on a wire rack
8. Cover and chill at least 3 hours

Run a knife around edge of flan to loosen; invert onto a serving plate.

Classic Cheesecake

Ingredients:

Butter Crunch Crust:
- ½ cup all-purpose flour
- ¼ cup finely chopped pecans or walnuts
- 2 Tablespoons brown sugar
- 4 Tablespoons (½ stick) unsalted butter, at room temperature

Filling:
- 1½ pounds cream cheese, at room temperature, cut into small pieces
- 1¼ cups sugar
- ¼ teaspoon salt
- ¾ cup sour cream
- 1 Tablespoon dark rum
- 1 Tablespoon lemon juice
- 2 Tablespoons vanilla extract
- 3 eggs

Garnish:
- fresh berries

continued on next page

continued from previous page

Directions:

1. Position the rack in the center of the oven and preheat the oven to 350° F. Coat the bottom of a 9-inch or 10-inch springform pan with butter or nonstick spray

2. In a large bowl, assemble all the ingredients for the Butter Crunch Crust. Mix them together with your hands until the mixture resembles very small pebbles

3. Press the crust into the bottom of the springform pan, covering the base completely and evenly. Wrap heavy-duty aluminum foil, or two layers of regular foil, around the outside of the pan's bottom and halfway up its side, pleating the foil to tighten it securely. Bake the crust until it is lightly golden, about 8 minutes. Remove from the oven and set aside.

4. To make the filling: Put the cream cheese, sugar, and salt in the large bowl of an electric stand mixer fitted with a paddle or beaters, or in a large mixing bowl. Using the stand mixer or a handled mixer on medium speed, beat the ingredients until smooth, stopping often to scrape down the sides of the bowl and under the blades with a rubber spatula. Turn the speed high and continue to beat until mixture is creamy. Stop the mixer and add the sour cream, rum, lemon juice, and vanilla; then, on medium speed, continue beating until well-blended. Add the eggs and beat just until combined. Scrape the filling into the prepared springform pan.

5. Bring a kettle of water to a boil. Place the springform pan inside a slightly larger baking pan. Using an oven glove, pull out the oven shelf and place the baking pan on it. Pour enough hot water into the pan to reach halfway up the sides of the springform pan, but not above the foil. Carefully slide the shelf into the oven and bake the cheesecake until its top is slightly golden and slightly firm in the center, about 1 hour and 10 minutes.

6. Carefully remove the baking pan from the oven. Lift out the springform pan and place it on a wire rack to cool, carefully folding down the foil on its sides to promote quicker cooling. When the pan is cool enough to touch, completely remove the foil and continue cooling. When the cheesecake is completely cool, cover the pan loosely with a clean sheet of foil and refrigerate overnight.

7. When ready to serve, remove the cheesecake from the refrigerator. Dip a long, sharp knife in warm water and run the knife around the inside of the springform pan to loosen the cake. Remove the outer ring. Continue to dip the knife into warm water as necessary as you cut neat wedges. To serve, place a wedge of cake on a cake plate and garnish with fresh berries of your choice. Or, for a special end to a meal, cover the entire cheesecake with assorted fresh berries and present it that way at the table before slicing and serving

Cherry Crescent Cheesecake Cups

highly recommended by Jane Westley and Esther Gallagher

Makes 8 servings

Ingredients:

- Cups:
    - 8-oz. can Pillsbury™ refrigerated Crescent Dinner Rolls™
- Filling:
    - 8-oz. package cream cheese, softened
    - 1 egg
    - 2 cups confectioners' sugar
    - ¼ cup chopped almonds, pecans, or walnuts
    - 1 teaspoon almond extract
- Topping:
    - 2 cups (1 lb. 5-oz. can) cherry pie filling
    - ¼ cup lemon juice or Kirsch
    - 1 Tablespoon butter

Directions:

1. Pre-heat oven to 350* F

Filling Preparation:

1. In a small mixer bowl, blend cream cheese and egg together
2. Add confectioners' sugar, chopped nuts, and almond extract, and mix well
3. Set aside

Cup Preparation:

1. Lightly grease 8 muffin cups
2. Separate Crescent Dough into 4 rectangles. Firmly press perforations in dough rectangles to seal and prevent dough separation during baking
3. Roll out each rectangle into a 10 x 5-inch rectangle. Cut each rectangle in half, making eight 5 x 5-inch squares
4. Place about ¼ cup of filling in each square
5. Bring 4 corners of the square together; place in the muffin cup and seal the dough edges facing up in the muffin cup
6. Bake for 18 to 22 minutes until golden brown

Topping Preparation:

1. In medium saucepan, combine all topping ingredients
2. Cook over low heat until bubbly and butter melts, stirring occasionally

When filled crescents have finished baking, immediately remove them from the muffin pan and serve warm with your topping

Grammie Jane's 4-Layer Cheesecake

I have made this a number of times but one comes to mind in particular. At a Gallagher Thanksgiving gathering, Elise told all the kids how good this is. They all came in from playing outside and asked for a piece of my 4-Layer Cheesecake. They finished the cheesecake before any adults had a chance for a taste. I only recommend taking a small piece, as this is very rich.

Preparation time: 4 hours
Inactivetime: 3 hours
Cooking time: 30 minutes
Yield: 12 servings

Ingredients:
- Layer 1: Chocolate Cake "Crust":
    - ½ cup salted butter, softened, plus more for greasing
    - 1 cup sugar
    - 1 teaspoon Mexican vanilla extract
    - 3 eggs
    - ½ cup all-purpose flour
    - ⅓ cup Dutch-process baking cocoa
- Layer 2: Baked Chocolate Cheesecake:
    - 8 ounces cream cheese, softened
    - ½ cup ricotta cheese
    - ¾ cup sugar
    - 1 ounce unsweetened chocolate, melted and cooled (or packaged pre-melted)
    - 2 eggs
    - 1 Tablespoon all-purpose flour
- Layer 3: Vanilla Cream Cheese Mousse:
    - 1½ cups heavy cream
    - 8 ounces cream cheese
    - ½ cup sugar
    - 2 teaspoons Mexican vanilla extract
- Layer 4: Dark Chocolate/White Chocolate Ganache:
    - 10 ounces dark chocolate, chopped, or about 1½ cups dark chocolate chips
    - 1 cup heavy whipping cream
    - 2 Tablespoons butter
    - ¼ cup white chocolate chips
    - 1½ cups chocolate chips for garnish

continued on next page

continued from previous page

Directions:

1. For **the chocolate cake "crust":** Preheat the oven to 350° F. Lightly grease the bottom only of a 9-inch springform pan that has been lined with parchment paper. In a medium bowl, cream together the butter and sugar. Add the vanilla and eggs, beating well Add the flour and cocoa and mix well to combine. The batter will be stiff. Spread in the pan. Set aside.

2. For **the baked chocolate cheesecake:** In a large bowl, cream the cream cheese and ricotta with the sugar until smooth. Add a small amount of the cheese mixture to the melted chocolate and combine well. Once the little bit of cheese mixture and chocolate is mixed well, add it back to the rest of the cheese mixture and beat until well combined. Add the eggs and flour and beat well. Smooth over the top of the cake batter in the pan. Bake until the cheesecake is set in the center, 25 to 30 minutes. Cover with foil during last 10 minutes of baking to prevent over browning. Remove from the oven and cool. **I recommend stopping here, cleaning up, and refrigerating over night**. After you chill the cheesecake it will set without wobbling.

3. For **the vanilla cream cheese mousse:** Once your chocolate and cheesecake base has been chilled, you can start making the third layer. Beat the heavy whipping cream until stiff and set aside. In separate bowl, beat the cream cheese, sugar, and vanilla with a mixer in large bowl until well blended. Fold the whipped cream into cheese mixture until just combined. Spread the mixture over the baked cheesecake layer and chill well (freezing the cake at this point works well and makes spreading the final layer easier). Make sure you chill for several hours to make sure all the layers are set.

4. For **the dark chocolate/white chocolate ganache:** Place the chopped dark chocolate in a large bowl. Heat the cream and butter over low heat until just boiling. Reserve 2 Tablespoons of the cream mixture. Pour the rest of the cream mixture over the chocolate and let set about 2 minutes, or until it begins to melt. Stir to combine. Repeat for the white chips using the reserved cream mixture. Let cool slightly until it reaches spreading consistency.

5. Using a sharp knife, gently run the blade around the edge of the cake to loosen. Remove the cake sides from the pan and place the bottom with cake on a serving plate or stand. Spread the frosting over the top and sides.

6. Drizzle the white chocolate lightly over the top. Using a knife or toothpick, run it lightly over the top to swirl to create desired effect. At this point, I would place the white chocolate ganache in a pastry bag and use a small round tip to decorate the top of the cake instead of trying to just drizzle it on top. That way you have more control.

7. Press the chocolate chips into the frosting on sides. Place the cake in the refrigerator to chill

Serve and Enjoy!

Lisa's Triple Rich Chocolate Cake

Makes 8 to 10 servings

Ingredients:

- 1 box Devil's Food cake mix
- 4 eggs
- 1 cup light sour cream
- ¾ cup vegetable oil
- 1 cup water
- 1 package instant chocolate pudding
- 1 cup chocolate chips

Directions:

1. Combine all ingredients **by hand** (not using a mixer) in a 2-quart mixing bowl
2. Pour batter into greased 3½ to 5-quart slow cooker
3. Cover and cook on **low heat** 5 to 6 hours, or until done in the center

Chef Note:

- Do not cook this recipe on high heat

Molten Chocolate Cake

A Valentine's Day treat for the senses!

Enjoy and be rewarded with the rich chocolaty scent, the decadent taste and the surprise of seeing a river of warm chocolate pour out when you cut into them.

Serves 4

Ingredients:

- ½ cup (1 stick) butter, plus more for buttering the molds
- 4 ounces bittersweet chocolate
- 2 eggs
- 2 egg yolks
- ¼ cup sugar
- 2 teaspoons flour, plus more for dusting
- 2 Tablespoons confectioners' sugar

Directions:

1. In the top of a double boiler set over simmering water, heat the butter and chocolate together until the chocolate is almost completely melted
2. While the chocalate is heating, beat together the eggs, egg yolks, and sugar with a whisk or electric beater until light and thick
3. Beat together the melted chocolate and butter; it should be quite warm. Pour in the egg mixture, and then quickly beat in the flour, just until combined
4. Butter and lightly flour four 4-ounce molds, custard cups. or ramekins. Tap out the excess flour, then butter and flour them again. Divide the batter among the molds (at this point you can refrigerate the desserts until you are ready to eat, for up to several hours; bring them back to room temperate before baking)
5. Preheat the oven to 450° F
6. Bake the molds on a tray for 6 to 7 minutes; the center will still be quite soft, but the sides will set
7. Invert each mold onto a plate and let sit for about 10 seconds. Unmold by carefully lifting up one corner of the mold; the cake should fall out onto the plate
8. Sprinkle with confectioners' sugar and serve immediately. Recommend serving with a scoop of vanilla ice cream and some berries

Deb and Jane's Crème Brûlée

You will ideally use a culinary butane torch or you may need to borrow a plumbing torch.

Makes 8 servings

Ingredients:

    7 large eggs

    ¾ cup granulated sugar

    4 cups heavy cream

    1 teaspoon vanilla extract or 1 vanilla bean

    ¼ teaspoon salt

    ¾ cup granulated sugar for the top

    Optional topping of berries and confectioners' sugar

Directions:

1. Pre-heat your oven to 300° F. Heat a kettle of water for the hot water bath. Place eight baking dishes (ramekins) in a large roasting pan.

2. In a medium sauce pan combine the cream, half of the sugar (¼ cup plus 2 Tablespoons), and vanilla. Heat over medium heat just until the mixture starts to bubble around the edges, approx. 7 to 8 minutes. **Do not let boil!**

3. Separate the egg yolks into a large mixing bowl

4. Using a whisk beat the yolks for a minute until they're completely smooth. Add the other half of the sugar (¼ cup plus 2 Tablespoons) and salt and continue to whisk for about 2 more minutes, until the sugar is fully incorporated and the yolks are a pale shade of yellow.

5. Temper the egg mixture by using a ladle to add a small amount of the hot cream mixture and whisk to combine. Continue adding a ladle of cream and whisking each time until fully incorporated

continued on next page

continued from previous page

6. Strain the custard through a fine sieve into a large liquid measuring cup to remove any solids

7. Carefully pour the custard into the ramekins. Fill all the ramekins about halfway; then, top up each one a little at a time so they are equally full and you won't run out of custard

8. Now transfer the roasting pan to the oven. Fill the roasting pan about halfway up the ramekins with hot water

9. Bake for 35 minutes or until the edges are set but the centers just barely jiggle when you nudge the pan

10. Remove the pan from the oven. Use tongs to carefully remove the ramekins from the hot water bath to a wire rack for cooling for 30 minutes. Then cover the ramekins with plastic and chill for at least 2 hours or up to 3 days before serving

11. About 20 minutes before serving, take the ramekins out of the refrigerator and let them sit at room temperature

12. Caramelize the tops by sprinkling about 1½ Tablespoons of sugar over each custard. Be generous, making sure you cover the whole surface

13. It's time for the *brûlée* — which means, "burnt" in French. Fire up your torch! Working one at a time, pass the flame of the torch in a circular motion 1 to 2 inches above the surface of each custard until the sugar bubbles, turns amber, and forms a smooth surface

14. You can serve the *crème brûlées* just as they are, and they'll be absolutely delicious. But a few fresh berries and a dusting of confectioners' sugar is a nice, elegant touch.

Chef Notes:
- This was D'Gall's signature dessert
- I put a tea towel in the roasting pan to keep the ramekins from moving around
- This recipe is not as hard as it looks. Try it — you will love it!

Crème Brûlée Bread Pudding

Ingredients:

    1 cup unsalted butter

    1 cup packed brown sugar

    2 Tablespoons corn syrup

    6 large croissants

    5 large eggs

    1½ cups half-and-half

    1 teaspoon vanilla

    1 teaspoon Grand Marnier

    ¼ teaspoon salt

Directions:

1. In a small saucepan, melt butter with brown sugar and corn syrup over medium heat, stirring until smooth
2. Pour into a 13 x 9-inch glass baking dish
3. Tear croissants into small pieces an inch or two in size and arrange in one layer, squeezing them slightly, to fill the dish on top of the syrup layer
4. In a bowl, whisk together eggs, half-and-half, vanilla, Grand Marnier, and salt until combined. and pour evenly over croissants
5. Cover dish with plastic wrap and chill in the refrigerator at least 8 hours or up to one day
6. Take out of refrigerator and let warm to room temperature while oven preheats to 350°F
7. Bake uncovered in middle of the oven until it pops up and looks golden brown on top, approximately 35 to 40 minutes

Lisa and Lori's Enchanted Castle Cake

Ingredients:
- 1 box of your favorite cake mix
- 1 can fluffy white frosting
- 2 wafer ice cream cones (pointy ones)
- Decorative cake sugar or sprinkles
- 1 box pillow mints
- 1 Hershey™ candy bar

Directions:
1. Cover a large piece of cardboard with foil or use a really big tray
2. Using your favorite cake mix follow directions on cake mix and bake as directed in a 13 x 9½ inch cake pan. Cool 10 minutes
3. Remove cake from pan and allow cake to be completely cooled
4. Cut Cake In The Following Manner:
    - Cut cake in half crosswise into two 8 x 6 rectangles. Place one piece on your foil tray to become your base.
    - Cut other half cake section into 3 equal pieces, each about 6 x 2½ inches
    - Cut one of these pieces in half to make 2 small squares
    - With a sharp knife trim the 2 small squares into round pieces. These are your towers for the cake.
5. Cover the base piece of cake with fluffy white frosting
6. Place the 2 remaining larger rectangles on left and right sides of the base layer and frost
7. Place the rounded remaining cakes on the corners of the base cake and frost.
8. Take 2 wafer ice cream cones and trim them to fit the top of the rounded cake. Frost the cones and roll in colored sugar. Place these decorated cones upside done (point up) on top of rounded towers.
9. Make flags out of toothpicks and construction paper. Place on top of cones and on top of cake.
10. Use little pillow mints and decorate top of cake like a stonewall.
11. Break up a Hershey bar to add the windows and doors for your wonderful ENCHANTED CASTLE!

Now decide how you want to attack your Enchanted Castle!

Fastnachts
(Pennsylvania Dutch/German Yeast Doughnuts)

Fastnacht Day is a special Pennsylvania Dutch celebration that falls on Shrove Tuesday, the day before Ash Wednesday. The word translates to 'Fast Night'. The tradition is to eat the very best, and lots of it, before the Lenten fast. Fastnachts (pronounced fost-nokts) are doughnuts. Traditionally, all Fastnachts were made with lard, and fried in it.

Makes 4 to 5 dozen

Ingredients:

Sponge:

- 2 cups milk, room temperature
- 1 package (2¼ teaspoons) rapid-rise dry yeast
- ¼ cup lukewarm water
- 1 teaspoon granulated sugar
- 3 cups all-purpose flour

Dough:

- 2 large eggs, room temperature
- ⅓ cup vegetable shortening (preferably non-hydrogenated)
- 3 cups all-purpose flour, more if needed
- 1 teaspoon salt
- 1 teaspoon ground nutmeg
- ¾ cup granulated sugar
- Vegetable or canola oil for frying, about 2 quarts

Directions:

For the sponge:

1. Scald the milk, but do not boil, and cool
2. Dissolve the yeast in the water and let rest until it starts to bubble to make certain it is alive
3. Place the milk, 1 teaspoon sugar, 3 cups flour, and yeast mixture in the large bowl of an electric mixer. Stir on low just until combined
4. Cover and let rise in a draft-free area until doubled, about 30 minutes

continued on next page

continued from previous page

For the dough:

1. Beat the eggs in a small bowl. Melt the shortening and let cool

2. When the sponge has doubled, add the eggs, melted shortening, and the ¾ cup sugar; stir just to combine

3. Place 3 cups of flour in a medium bowl. Add the salt and nutmeg; stir with a whisk to combine

4. On the lowest setting of the mixer add the flour mixture, about one-third at a time. Stir just to combine. Do not overmix. The dough should be very soft and just dry enough to roll. If it is very sticky, incorporate just a little more flour, about 2 Tablespoons at a time

5. Cover and let rise until doubled, 1½ to 2 hours

6. When doubled, place dough on a lightly floured surface. Gently roll to about ½-inch thickness, as close to a square or rectangle as possible

7. Cut into 2-inch squares. If desired, cut a slit down the center of each square, being careful not to go all the way through the dough. (This is traditional for Fastnachts. Supposedly, it makes them crispier all over the outside, but it is not necessary.) Place on large baking sheets lined with parchment or waxed paper. Cover and let rise again until nearly doubled, about 1½ to 2 hours

To fry doughnuts:

1. Place the oil in a deep pan high enough to hold the oil half way up the sides. Heat to 360°F over medium heat. Carefully fry the doughnuts, about 5 to 7 at a time, until well-browned on one side, about 3 minutes. Flip to other side and brown another 3 minutes. Remove from oil and drain on paper towels.

Notes:

- Doughnuts may be sprinkled with granulated or confectioners' sugar while still warm

- The PA Dutch tradition is to cut the doughnut open horizontally and drizzle the cut sides with molasses or corn syrup

- They are best served the same day because they are so good when warm and crispy; however, they are still good stored in plastic bags in the refrigerator for up to a week, or in the freezer for several months. Leftover Fastnachts are best placed in a preheated 350°F oven for about 5 minutes to recrisp slightly

Wilson Fruit Cobbler

This is so easy, but gosh is it good with some vanilla ice cream!

Ashley Edwards

Ingredients:

- ¼ cup butter
- 1 cup flour
- 1¾ cups sugar
- 2 teaspoons baking powder
- ½ teaspoons salt
- ¾ cup milk
- 2 to 3 cups fresh berries (blackberries are my preference)

Directions:

1. Preheat the oven to 350° F
2. Melt butter in 9-inch square pan
3. Combine flour, ¾ cup sugar, baking powder, salt, and milk
4. Pour the batter over the butter
5. Spread berries over the batter. Sprinkle the additional cup of granulated sugar over the berries
6. Bake until batter comes to the top and there is a golden-brown crust. (I start checking every few minutes after about 35 minutes.)

Note:
- Sometimes the juices bubble over, so it's a good idea to put a piece of foil on a lower rack beneath the baking cobbler

Key Lime Pie

Ingredients:

Crust:

⅓ of a 1-pound box graham crackers

5 Tablespoons melted, unsalted butter

⅓ cup sugar

Pie Filling:

4 egg yolks

2 teaspoons lime zest - be sure to zest before you squeeze the juice!

14-ounce can sweetened condensed milk

⅔ cup freshly squeezed lime juice (approximately 12 to 16 key limes, or 6 to 8 regular limes)

Meringue Topping:

4 egg whites

¼ teaspoon cream of tartar

2 Tablespoons confectioners' sugar

continued on next page

continued from previous page

Directions:

For crust:

1. Preheat the oven to 350°F

2. Make the graham cracker pie crust by breaking up the graham cracker, then add the melted butter and sugar, mix or stir until combined

3. Lightly press the mixture into the bottom and up the sides of a 9-inch pie pan. Bake the crust at 350°F for 8 minutes until set and golden. Set aside on a wire rack and let cool

For filling:

1. Using a rasp, grate the lime peel

2. Using a hand press, squeeze lime juice by cutting each lime in half and placing in press

3. Separate the egg yolks from the whites. Set aside the egg whites for the meringue

4. In an electric mixer with the wire whisk attachment, beat the egg yolks and lime zest at high speed until very fluffy, about 5 minutes

5. Gradually add the condensed milk and continue to beat until thick, 3 or 4 minutes

6. Lower the mixer speed and slowly add the lime juice, mixing just until combined

7. Pour the mixture into the crust. Bake at 350°F for 10 minutes, or until the filling has just set. Cool on a wire rack.

For meringue:

1. With a mixer, beat egg whites with cream of tartar until soft peaks form

2. Gradually beat in the sugar until stiff peaks form

3. Spread over filling and seal to edge of crust

4. Bake at 400°F for 5 - 8 minutes or until meringue is golden brown

5. Place in the refrigerator and let it chill for 2-3 hours.

Notes:

- Watch the oven and don't take your eyes off the meringue — it could brown quickly

- If you prefer, whipped cream can be substituted for the meringue topping

Mom's Lemon Sponge Pie

Ingredients:

    3 cups sugar

    3 lemon rinds, grated

    6 Tablespoons flour

    3 Tablespoons melted butter

    4 eggs

    3 cups milk

Directions:

1. Use your own pie dough recipe to make 2 - 3 pie crusts
2. Mix first four ingredients
3. Separate eggs
4. Add yolks to milk and add to first four ingredients
5. Beat egg whites and fold in last
6. Add mixture to pie pans with crusts
7. Bake at 300° F for 1 hour

Pie should be a lemony cream underneath with a cakey top crust made from egg whites. Enjoy!

Brenda's Mandarin Orange Cake

Ingredients:

Cake:

    2 eggs
    2 cups flour
    2 cups sugar
    2 teaspoons baking soda
    ½ teaspoon salt
    2 11-oz. cans mandarin oranges with juice

Topping:

    ¾ cup brown sugar
    3 Tablespoons milk
    2 Tablespoons butter

Directions:

1. Mix the cake ingredients together and beat until smooth
2. Put in a 13 x 9 x 2 well-greased baking pan
3. Bake at 350° F for 25 to 30 minutes
4. Bring topping ingredients to a boil and pour on top of the baked cake

Serve and Enjoy!

Grilled Peaches with Chocolate

Ingredients:

    4 large freestone peaches (2 pounds)

    2 Tablespoons sweet butter, softened

    2 ounces semi-sweet or milk chocolate, from a bar, cut into 8 pieces

    1 pint premium vanilla ice cream

Directions:

1. Preheat grill or broiler
2. Cut peaches in half and remove pits
3. Rub softened butter all over skin sides and cut sides of peaches
4. Place on grill, cut side down, over medium high heat. Grill 4 minutes, until golden
5. Turn peaches carefully with a pair of tongs. Grill on skin side for 4 more minutes, until golden. Turn off the grill
6. Place one piece of chocolate on each cut side of grilled peach. Cover them in the grill for one minute, until chocolate is melted
7. Portion ice cream evenly among 4 dessert bowls. Top each serving with 2 peach halves

Lisa's Peanut Butter Tandy Cake

Ingredients:

    4 eggs

    2 cups white sugar

    1 teaspoon vanilla extract

    2 cups flour

    1 teaspoon baking powder

    1 cup milk

    2 Tablespoons margarine

    1¼ cups peanut butter (either creamy or crunchy)

    2-pound milk chocolate candy bar, chopped

Directions:

1. Preheat oven to 350° F
2. In a large bowl, combine eggs, sugar, and vanilla, and beat with an electric mixer on high speed until light and lemony-colored
3. Beat in the flour mixture
4. Microwave milk and margarine about 2 minutes, or until it beings to bubble, and stir into batter
5. Pour batter into 10 x 15 inch pan
6. Bake in preheated oven for 20 - 25 minutes, or until a toothpick inserted into the center of the cake comes out clean
7. Spread the peanut butter shortly after the cake comes out of the oven, as it melts and is easy to smooth. Let cool
8. In a microwave safe dish, melt chocolate and spread evenly over peanut butter layer
9. Refrigerate to allow chocolate to harden

Pie Crust

Ingredients:

    2 cups sifted all-purpose flour

    ⅓ cup shortening, chilled

    ⅓ cup butter, chilled (5⅓ Tablespoons stick butter cut into 1/16-inch thick pieces)

    dash of salt

    ¼ cup milk (add more if needed)

    1 egg and 2 Tablespoons water beaten together to make egg wash

Directions:

1. Combine flour, shortening, butter, and salt in power mixer until it resembles coarse crumbs
2. Add milk 1 Tablespoon at a time, tossing crumb mixture until the ingredients cling together
3. Coat work surface with dusting of flour, press dough together, and cut into two portions
4. Wrap dough in plastic wrap and chill for at least an hour
5. On a lightly floured board, roll pie dough into a circular sheet approximately ⅛ inch thick large enough to fit a 9-inch pie pan
6. Transfer dough sheet to pie pan by rolling it up on rolling pin and unrolling over pie pan. Press dough sheet into pie pan leaving ½ inch of dough above the pan edge
7. Fill pie pan with pie centers
8. Roll out second circle of pie dough, leaving an extra ½ inch of dough
9. Use egg wash to coat dough edges and pinch both layers of dough together
10. Cut a few slits across the center of the top dough to let steam out
11. Brush the top crust lightly with the egg wash.

Pumpkin Pie

Ingredients:

    2 large eggs, slightly beaten

    2 cups cooked, mashed pumpkin or 1 regular size can Libby's™ pumpkin

    ¾ cup sugar

    ½ teaspoon salt

    2 Tablespoons pumpkin pie spice

    1⅔ cups evaporated milk (13 oz. can)

    9¾-inch deep dish frozen pie shell, thawed or two regular frozen pie shells, thawed

Directions:

1. Combine ingredients in order given
2. Pour into pie shells. Place pie tins on cookie sheet(s)
3. Bake at 425° F for 15 minutes, then reduce heat to 350° F and bake an additional 30 minutes or until knife inserted near the center comes out clean

Note:
- Put aluminum foil around edge of pie crust to keep it from over-browning

Festive Pumpkin Pie

Ingredients:

- 8 oz. cream cheese, softened
- 1 teaspoon ground cinnamon
- ½ teaspoon salt
- 3 large eggs
- 1 cup milk
- 1 unbaked 9-inch pie shell
- 2 Tablespoons sugar
- ¾ cup brown sugar, firmly packed
- ½ teaspoon ground ginger
- ¼ teaspoon ground cloves
- 1 cup canned, mashed pumpkin
- 1 teaspoon vanilla
- 1 cup sour cream

Directions:

1. Using an electric mixer set on medium speed, cream the cheese, brown sugar, spices, and salt until they are light and fluffy. Add the eggs, one at a time, beating well after each addition. Blend in the pumpkin, milk, and vanilla

2. Pour the mixture into the unbaked pie shell. Bake in a preheated 375° F oven for 45 to 50 minutes or until a knife inserted halfway between the edge and center comes out clean. Cool slightly on a wire rack

3. Meanwhile, blend the sour cream and sugar together and spread over the top of the warm pie

4. Return the pie to the oven and bake an additional 3 to 5 minutes or just until the topping is set. Cool on a wire rack

5. Cool and chill in the refrigerator several hours before serving

Shana's Rhubarb Crumble

Ingredients:

Filling;
- 2 lbs. rhubarb
- 4 oz. brown sugar
- 1 heaping teaspoon grated fresh ginger

Crumble:
- 4 oz. whole almonds
- 3 oz. chilled butter, cut into thin slices
- 6 oz. sifted self-rising flour
- 2 teaspoons ground cinnamon
- 1 teaspoon ground ginger
- 4 oz. brown sugar

Directions:

Filling:

1. Prepare rhubarb by washing it, then trim off the leaves and cut the stalks roughly into 1-inch chunks
2. Toss cut rhubarb in a bowl and coat with the sugar and freshly grated ginger. Let mixture macerate.

Crumble:

1. Add almonds to a food processor and pulse until they are finely chopped; set aside.
2. Add butter, sifted flour, cinnamon, ground ginger, and sugar into a food processor. Pulse until mixture resembles crumbs. Next, add the chopped almonds and process again to combine into the crumble
3. Coat large casserole dish with cooking spray and spread rhubarb pieces evenly over bottom of the dish. Press the rhubarb firmly with your hands into the bottom of the dish to eliminate any large lumps
4. Sprinkle crumble mixture over the rhubarb, spreading it right up to the edges of the dish. Again use the flat of your hands to firmly press crumble down onto the rhubarb (the more tightly the crumble is packed together the crisper it will be). Finish off by lightly running a fork all over the surface
5. Pre-heat oven to 400° F. Place rhubarb dish on the center shelf in the oven and bake for 35 to 40 minutes, by which time the topping will be golden brown and crispy
6. Remove and let rest for 10 to 15 minutes before serving

   Suggest serving warm with ice cream, desert topping or prepared custard

Brenda's Rice Pudding

With consulting credits to June Moyer

Ingredients:

    8 cups milk

    ¾ cup regular rice

    1½ cups sugar

    2 eggs

    1 teaspoon vanilla

Directions:

1. Bring milk, sugar, and rice to a boil while stirring continuously in a heavy saucepan over medium-high heat
2. Cut temperature back to low heat
3. Stir every 15 minutes for one-and-a-half hours until it turns tan
4. Beat two eggs with ½ cup milk and vanilla
5. Put small amount of hot pudding into the egg mixture and stir, then put this mixture into the large pot of rice pudding and stir

Allow to cool and serve

Lisa's Sponge Cake

Ingredients:

- 3 eggs
- 1 teaspoon baking powder
- 1 cup sugar
- 3 Tablespoons warm water
- 1 cup flour
- 1 teaspoon lemon juice
- ½ teaspoon salt

Directions:

1. Beat the eggs until thick and creamy
2. Add sifted sugar and beat well
3. Add water and lemon juice and beat again
4. Sift the flour, add salt and baking powder, and sift again
5. Combine dry ingredients with the egg mixture by pouring a little bit at a time, folding in gently
6. When well-blended, pour into an ungreased pan with center tube
7. Bake at 350°F for 50 minutes

Joyce's Tapioca Pudding

Ingredients:

    2 quarts milk

    1 cup tapioca pearls

    1 to 1½ cups sugar

    4 eggs

    2 teaspoons vanilla

Directions:

    Follow the box directions for soaking the tapioca pearls

    Add the first 3 ingredients into a crock pot

    Heat on high for 3 hours

    Beat eggs and vanilla and stir in a little of the cooking tapioca

    Stir the eggs and vanilla mixture slowly into the crock pot

    Cook an additional 15 minutes

Some crockpots only take 2 hours. ENJOY!

Texas Sheet Cake

Ingredients:

Cake:

- 2 cups sugar
- 2 cups flour, sifted
- 2 sticks butter
- 4 Tablespoons cocoa
- 1 cup water
- ½ cup sour cream
- 1 teaspoon baking soda
- 1 teaspoon vanilla
- 2 eggs

Icing:

- 6 Tablespoons evaporated milk
- 4 Tablespoons cocoa
- 2 sticks butter
- 3 cups confectioners' sugar
- 1 cup chopped nuts
- 1 teaspoon vanilla

Directions:

Cake:

1. Bring water to a boil on top of stove or in microwave
2. Mix all ingredients together
3. Bake at 350° F for 25 to 30 minutes in a 13 x 9-inch pan

Icing:

1. Melt butter on top of stove or in microwave
2. Mix all ingredients together

Cookies

Lisa's Banana Bars

Ingredients:

- ¼ cup shortening
- 1 cup sugar
- 2 eggs
- 1 cup mashed banana
- 1 teaspoon vanilla
- 2 cups flour
- 2 teaspoons baking powder
- ½ teaspoon salt

Directions:

1. Preheat oven to 350° F
2. Grease a 15 x 10-inch jelly roll pan
3. Thoroughly mix shortening, sugar, eggs, bananas, and vanilla
4. Sift flour and mix in dry ingredients
5. Stir dry ingredients into banana mixture
6. Spread in prepared pan
7. Bake 20 to 25 minutes, or until golden brown

Erica's Buckeyes

Ingredients:

1½ cups creamy peanut butter

1 cup butter, softened

6 cups powdered sugar

1 teaspoon vanilla

½ teaspoon salt

4 cups semi-sweet chocolate chips

2 Tablespoons all-vegetable shortening

Directions:

1. Combine peanut butter, butter, vanilla, and salt in large bowl. Beat with an electric mixer on **low** until blended
2. Add 5 cups of powdered sugar slowly, beating until blended and dough ball forms
3. Beat in additional powdered sugar until mixture, when shaped into a ball, will stay on a toothpick
4. Shape into 1-inch balls and place on wax paper-lined tray. Freeze for 20 to 30 minutes until firm
5. Place chocolate chips and shortening in microwave-safe bowl. Microwave on **medium** for 30 seconds. Stir. Repeat until mixture is smooth. Reheat chocolate as needed while coating peanut butter balls
6. Insert toothpick in peanut butter ball. Dip ¾ of ball into chocolate, leaving top uncovered to resemble a buckeye. Remove excess chocolate
7. Place on wax paper-lined tray and remove toothpick. Smooth over holes
8. Refrigerate until firm

Salted Caramel Snickerdoodles

Ingredients:

    Bag of caramels, unwrapped

    1 pouch Snickerdoodle cookie mix

    Butter, egg, and water, as called for on cookie mix pouch

    ½ teaspoon salt

Directions:

1. Line cookie sheet with parchment paper
2. Heat oven to 375° F
3. Make cookie dough as directed on cookie mix pouch
4. Shape heaping Tablespoons of dough into balls. Using lightly-floured hands, press thumb into center of each cookie to make deep indentation, but do not press all the way through
5. Place a caramel into center of each cookie, making sure to form dough around the caramel to enclose. If necessary, work with lightly-floured fingers so dough doesn't stick
6. In small bowl, mix cinnamon sugar mixture from cookie pouch and the salt and roll balls in sugar mixture
7. Place 3 inches apart on cookie sheets
8. Bake 10 to 12 minutes or until set (centers will be soft).
9. Cool 2 minutes on cooking sheet.
10. Remove from cookie sheet to cooling rack.

Aunt Marta's French Lace Cookies

Ingredients:

- 2 oz. blanched almonds (to yield ½ cup ground almonds)
- 5 Tablespoons (2½ oz.) unsalted butter
- ⅓ cup granulated sugar
- 2 Tablespoons light corn syrup
- ⅓ cup (1½ oz.) all-purpose flour
- 1 teaspoon vanilla
- Pinch salt

Directions:

1. Position two racks in the middle and upper third of the oven and preheat oven to 350° F. Line two baking sheets with nonstick liners or parchment paper
2. In a food processor, grind the almonds finely and measure out ½ cup
3. Heat the butter, sugar, and corn syrup in a medium saucepan over low heat, stirring often, until the butter melts and the sugar dissolves. Increase the heat to medium high and, stirring constantly, bring the mixture just to a boil. Remove the pot from the heat and stir in the flour and salt until incorporated
4. Stir in the ground almonds and the vanilla
5. Drop the batter by the teaspoon 3 inches apart on the baking sheets, about six cookies per baking sheet
6. Bake the cookies until evenly light brown, about 10 minutes total. About 5 minutes into baking, switch the sheets from top to bottom and back to front to promote even baking.

Note:
- The cookies won't begin to spread until about 6 minutes into baking

Grammie Jane's Island Cookies

Makes about 3 dozen cookies

Ingredients:

- 2¼ cups all purpose flour
- ½ teaspoon salt
- ¾ cup brown sugar
- 1 teaspoon vanilla extract
- 1 teaspoon baking soda
- 1 cup (2 sticks) butter
- ¾ cup white sugar
- 2 large eggs

- 2 cups white chocolate chips
- 1 cup dried cherries
- 1 cup flaked coconut
- ¾ cup chopped macadamia nuts

Directions:

1. Preheat oven to 375° F
2. Sift flour and combine with baking soda and salt in bowl
3. Beat butter, brown sugar, sugar, and vanilla in large mixer bowl until creamy. Beat in eggs
4. Gradually add and beat in flour mixture
5. Stir in chocolate chips, coconut, cherries, and macadamia nuts
6. Drop a Tablespoon scoop of cookie dough onto parchment-covered baking sheets and bake for 9 to 11 minutes or until edges are lightly browned
7. Remove from oven and let rest on baking sheets before transferring cookies to wire racks for complete cooling.

Notes:

- The Tollhouse Cookie™ recipe consists of the ingredients above the line
- Adjusting the remaining ingredients below the line gives you:
  - ★ Chocolate Chip Cookies, by substituting 2 cups chocolate chips
  - ★ Toffee Chip Cookies, by substituting 1 cup chocolate chips and 1 cup toffee chips
  - ★ Peanut Butter Chocolate Chip Cookies, by substituting 1 cup chocolate chips and 1 cup peanut butter chips
  - ★ Don't forget about adding chopped nuts, raisins, or cherries if that works for you.

Homemade Nutter Butters™

A Nutter Butter™ sandwich to enjoy!

Makes 6 cookie sandwiches

Ingredients:

Cookies:

- 1 cup sugar
- 1 cup peanut butter
- 1 egg

Filling:

- ¼ cup butter, at room temperature
- ¼ cup peanut butter, at room temperature
- 1 cup powdered sugar
- 1 to 2 Tablespoons milk

Directions:

Cookies:

1. Preheat the oven to 350° F
2. Stir the cookie ingredients together until smooth
3. Make the cookie dough into the shape of a Nutter Butter™ cookie, scoop out a one-inch ball of cookie dough and roll into a log shape
4. Press down with the back of a fork and then press again from the opposite direction to make the crisscross pattern on top of each cookie. Finish by pinching in both sides of each cookie before baking
5. Bake for 12 minutes and then let cool on the tray for 1 to 2 minutes more

Filling:

1. Beat the butter and peanut butter together in a large bowl with a hand mixer until smooth
2. Slowly add in the powdered sugar and beat until smooth
3. Add the milk, one Tablespoon at a time, until the desired consistency is reached
4. Spread a Tablespoon of the filling onto the bottom side of one of the cookies and then top with another cookie to create a cookie sandwich

Oatmeal Chocolate Chip Cookies
"Mom's Cowboy Cookies"

Ingredients:

- 2 cups rolled oats
- 2 cups sifted flour
- 1 teaspoon baking soda
- 1 teaspoon baking powder
- 1 cup shortening
- 1 cup brown sugar
- 1 cup granulated sugar
- 1 teaspoon vanilla extract
- 2 eggs
- 1 package semi-sweet chocolate bits
  - or use a mixture of chocolate, peanut butter, and butterscotch chips. You could also substitute chopped nuts, raisins, or dried cherries

Directions:

1. Preheat oven to 375*
2. Combine oats, flour, baking powder, and baking soda in bowl
3. Beat shortening, brown sugar, granulated sugar, and vanilla in large mixer bowl until creamy. Beat in eggs
4. Gradually add and beat in oat and flour mixture
5. Stir in chips
6. Drop rounded Tablespoons of batter onto parchment paper lined baking sheets
7. Bake for 8 to 10 minutes or until edges are lightly browned and centers soft
8. Cool on baking sheets for 2 minutes; then remove to wire racks to cool completely

Erica's Oreo™ Balls

Oreo™ balls are fun, easy to make with children. The Oreo™ ball will remind you of a chocolate truffle, but instead of a chocolate filling, you get a rich, decadent Oreo™ cream cheese filling. Oreo™ balls are insanely delicious!

Ingredients:

- 1 package Oreo™ chocolate cookies with white filling
- 8 oz. Philadelphia™ cream cheese
- 1 cup milk chocolate chips
- 1 cup white chocolate chips
- Favorite desert toppings; cookie sprinkles, chopped nuts, crushed Oreos™, chocolate, or others

Directions:

1. Place the Oreo™ cookies in a food processor and pulse until you have small cookie crumbs. Make sure there are no big cookie pieces
2. Make sure your cream cheese is soft. If it is too cold, it won't mix into the Oreo™ crumbs easily
3. Use a mixer to combine the Oreo™ crumbs and cream cheese
4. Roll the Oreo™ cream cheese mixture into small balls and place on a baking sheet or tray that has been lined with parchment paper or wax paper
5. Freeze the balls for 15 minutes. **You must freeze them** so you can dip them in chocolate. If you don't, you will have a mess
6. Melt the chocolate chips in the microwave in a small microwave safe bowl. Follow the instructions on the package. I like to do a mix of milk and white chocolate. You can do just one type of chocolate if you wish
7. Dip the balls into the melted chocolate, making sure the balls are completely covered. I like to use a fork to lift them out of the chocolate, then I shake them from side to side to remove the excess chocolate
8. Place the Oreo™ balls back on the lined baking sheet or tray. You can decorate the tops with a drizzle of extra chocolate, crushed Oreos™, sprinkles, or chopped nuts. Or you can leave them plain!
9. When they are all dipped and decorated, place the baking sheet or tray in the refrigerator and chill for at least an hour

Aunt Marta's No-Bake Peanut Butter Balls
DGall Loved These

> Tips on How to make Easy Peanut Butter Balls:
>
> Make sure the peanut butter balls are chilled when you dip them. It will make the process **much** easier! The chocolate will set up more quickly and the peanut butter balls will hold their shape when you dip and tap off the excess warm chocolate.
>
> I like to use Ghirardelli Melting Wafers™ most of all for dipping. They melt **so** smooth and taste delicious. You don't need to add an extra Tablespoon of butter or shortening into the chocolate to thin it out — it's just the perfect consistency!
>
> But . . . if you can't find the Ghirardelli™ wafers, you certainly can use chocolate chips, or even almond bark. Since chocolate chips are necessarily made for melting, this is where you can add a Tablespoon of shortening or butter into the chocolate to thin it out a little bit, making the dipping process easier.
>
> You can melt the chocolate in the microwave in 25-second increments, or over a double boiler.
>
> If the chocolate thickens up too much while you're dipping, melt it again for a few seconds until you reach the desired consistency.
>
> You can decorate these peanut butter balls with sprinkles, sea salt, or just drizzle some extra chocolate over top, like I do!
>
> When you dip the peanut butter balls in the chocolate, make sure to tap off all the excess chocolate you can. Then, when you place the dipped ball onto the parchment-lined sheet, use a toothpick and drag it around the base of the ball so it doesn't pool up at the bottom.

Ingredients:

- 1 cup creamy peanut butter
- 1 cup butter, room temperature
- 4 cups powdered sugar
- 1¼ cups crushed graham crackers
- 15 ounces semi-sweet chocolate (for melting)

Directions:

1. In the bowl of your stand mixer fitted with the paddle attachment combine the peanut butter and butter, mixing on medium speed until smooth
2. Turn mixer to low and add in the powdered sugar and graham cracker crumbs, mixing until evenly incorporated. Mixture will be thick
3. Using a small cookie scoop (about 1 Tablespoon), portion out the mixture and roll into balls. Place them on a large parchment lined baking sheet. Place the baking sheet in the refrigerator for at least 30 minutes to chill
4. In a medium bowl melt the chocolate in 25-second increments, stirring after each until smooth
5. Using a fork, dip each peanut butter ball into the melted chocolate, tapping off the excess. Place back on the parchment-lined baking sheet. Repeat with all balls
6. Drizzle any extra chocolate on top of the balls
7. Allow the chocolate to set before storing
8. Store at room temperature for up to 2 days, or refrigerated for up to a week

Chocolate-Peanut Butter Candy Bars

Ingredients:
- 24 crème-filled chocolate sandwich cookies
- 4 cups miniature marshmallows
- ¼ cup butter or margarine
- 1 cup semisweet chocolate chips (6 oz.)
- 14-oz. can sweetened condensed milk (not evaporated)
- 10-oz. bag peanut butter chips (1⅔ cups)
- ¼ cup creamy peanut butter
- 1 cup coarsely-chopped peanuts or favorite nuts
- 4 Nature Valley™ peanut butter crunchy granola bars (2 pouches from 8.9-oz box), crushed
- 1 teaspoon vegetable oil

Directions:
1. Line bottom and sides of 13x9-inch (3-quart) glass baking dish with foil, leaving foil hanging over 2 opposite sides of pan
2. Place cookies in food processor bowl with metal blade. Cover and process until cookies are finely chopped
3. In 2-quart saucepan, cook marshmallows and butter over low heat, stirring constantly until melted. Stir in chopped cookies and ¾ cup of the chocolate chips until well mixed. Press in bottom of baking dish
4. In medium microwavable bowl, microwave milk and peanut butter chips uncovered on high for 30 seconds. Stir; microwave 30 to 60 seconds longer, stirring every 30 seconds until smooth and creamy
5. Stir in peanut butter until smooth; then stir in peanuts and crushed granola bars
6. Spread mixture over chocolate layer. If peanut butter mixture starts to set, microwave uncovered on high for 15 to 30 seconds or until warm and spreadable
7. In small microwavable bowl, microwave remaining ¼ cup chocolate chips and the oil uncovered on high for 30 to 45 seconds or until chips are melted and can be stirred smooth
8. Drizzle chocolate diagonally over peanut butter layer
9. Refrigerate 30 minutes or until set
10. To cut bars, remove from pan using foil to lift. Cut into 8 rows by 4 rows. Store covered in cool place

Expert Tips:
- To easily crush granola bars, leave them in the pouches. Gently pound with meat mallet or rolling pin to break them up
- The cookies can be crushed by using a rolling pin to crumbling them in a large food-storage plastic bag

Brenda's Sugar Cookies

I've been making this recipe since 1956. There is now a powered buttermilk in the baking aisle but I haven't tried it.
Love, Brenda

Makes about 60 cookies

Ingredients:

6 to 7 cups flour (2 lbs)

3 cups sugar

2 teaspoons baking powder

1 teaspoon baking soda

1 teaspoon salt

2 eggs

2 cups buttermilk

1 teaspoon vanilla

1 cup melted shortening (not oil)

Directions:

1. Mix together flour, sugar, baking powder, baking soda, and salt
2. Add eggs, buttermilk, and vanilla
3. Add shortening
4. Drop by large spoonfuls onto a coated cookie sheet
5. Bake at 375° F for 15 minutes

Cool cookies and ice with frosting and sprinkles/colored sugar or coconut

Lisa's Whoopee Pies

Ingredients:

Pie cakes:

- 4 cups flour
- 2 cups sugar
- 2 teaspoons baking powder
- 2 eggs
- 1 cup sour milk
- ½ teaspoon salt
- 1 cup cocoa
- 2 teaspoons baking soda
- 1 cup shortening
- 2 egg yolks (save whites for filling)
- 1 cup hot water

Pie filling:

- 3½ cups sifted 10-x sugar
- 4 Tablespoons flour
- 1 teaspoons vanilla
- 1½ cups Crisco™
- 4 Tablespoons milk

Directions:

Pie cakes:

1. Preheat oven to 350° F
2. Mix ingredients as cake and bake as drop cookies
3. Use a teaspoon to drop dough on cookie sheet
4. Bake for 6 to 8 minutes
5. Remove cookies to cooling rack

Filling:

1. Use mixer to combine all ingredients into a sweet filling
2. Beat egg whites with 2 Tablespoons of 10X sugar until stiff
3. Fold stiff egg whites into filling
4. When cookies have cooled, put filling between 2 cookies and sandwich them together — you have a whoopee pie to enjoy!

Appendix: Conversion Chart

Liquid Measure

8 ounces =	1 cup
2 cups =	1 pint
16 ounces =	1 pint
4 cups =	1 quart
1 gill =	1/2 cup or 1/4 pint
2 pints =	1 quart
4 quarts =	1 gallon
31.5 gal =	1 barrel
3 tsp =	1 tbsp
2 tbsp =	1/8 cup or 1 fluid ounce
4 tbsp =	1/4 cup
8 tbsp =	1/2 cup
1 pinch =	1/8 tsp or less
1 tsp =	60 drops

Conversion of US Liquid Measure to Metric System

1 fluid oz =	29.573 milliliters
1 cup =	230 milliliters
1 quart =	.94635 liters
1 gallon =	3.7854 liters
.033814 fluid ounce =	1 milliliter
3.3814 fluid ounces =	1 deciliter
33.814 fluid oz or 1.0567 qt =	1 liter

Dry Measure

2 pints =	1 quart
4 quarts =	1 gallon
8 quarts =	2 gallons or 1 peck
4 pecks =	8 gallons or 1 bushel
16 ounces =	1 pound
2000 lbs. =	1 ton

Conversion of US Weight and Mass Measure to Metric System

.0353 ounces =	1 gram
1/4 ounce =	7 grams
1 ounce =	28.35 grams
4 ounces =	113.4 grams
8 ounces =	226.8 grams
1 pound =	454 grams
2.2046 pounds =	1 kilogram
.98421 long ton or 1.1023 short tons =	1 metric ton

Linear Measure

12 inches =	1 foot
3 feet =	1 yard
5.5 yards =	1 rod
40 rods =	1 furlong
8 furlongs (5280 feet) =	1 mile
6080 feet =	1 nautical mile

Conversion of US Linear Measure to Metric System

1 inch =	2.54 centimeters
1 foot =	.3048 meters
1 yard =	.9144 meters
1 mile =	1609.3 meters or 1.6093 kilometers
.03937 in =	1 millimeter
.3937 in =	1 centimeter
3.937 in =	1 decimeter
39.37 in =	1 meter
3280.8 ft or .62137 miles =	1 kilometer

To convert a Fahrenheit temperature to Centigrade, do the following:
a. Subtract 32   b. Multiply by 5   c. Divide by 9

To convert Centigrade to Fahrenheit do the following:
a. Multiply by 9   b. Divide by 5   c. Add 32

www.ingramcontent.com/pod-product-compliance
Lightning Source LLC
Chambersburg PA
CBHW080847020526
44118CB00037B/2271